OUTLAW PILOT

MORE ADVENTURES

OF

JIMMY "MIDNIGHT" ANDERSON

J.F. Anderson
Writer's Den

Tel: (604)248-6130   Fax: (604) 954-1487
P.O.Box 147, Parksville, BC, Canada, V9P 1R8

OUTLAW PILOT
PUBLISHED BY WRITERS DEN

ANDERSON, JAMES F., 1948-
OUTLAW PILOT
ISBN # 0-9697209-1-2

COVER PICTURE; "GATES OF THE PEACE"
PHOTOGRAPHS BY TOM REDHEAD
COMPUTER ILLUSIONS BY PAUL RUDYK

COMPUTER ASSISTANCE TIM L'HERAULT

ILLUSTRATIONS BY JIM ZINGER AND ROD
STEWART.

EDITING;
 LYLE ADAMS, MARILYN ANDERSON, IRENE
BESSEY

THANKS TO; KEITH MITCHELL AND ROGER YORK

GUIDANCE AND DIRECTION; EARL BROWN

PRINTED AND BOUND IN CANADA

CONTENTS

DEDICATED

TO

THOSE WHO HAVE WAITED

PROLOGUE

A bruptly, the ringing phone woke me. "Hello," I answered to the mechanical beckoning.

"Hello," answered a deep gruff voice, "I'm an old friend of your Dad." He was phoning at twenty minutes to midnight so I could see he had picked up one of Dad's habits. Turned out Gill lived in North Vancouver and owned a small gold mining operation on the west coast of Vancouver Island. Years ago he had worked the pipelines around Fort Nelson.

"Did you ever wonder how your old man managed to roar around the North country day or night and still hang onto his pilot's licence?" asked Gill in a confidential tone. "Thousands of flying hours were spent moving unconventional cargo ranging from trappers and their sled dogs to wild animals thrust in behind the pilot's seat," he stated. "Using whatever aircraft that was handy at the time, Jimmy flew whenever and wherever he wanted to in the North," continued Gill.

"Where do you think the Department of Transport was while all this was going on?" quizzed Gill. "Sleeping?? I doubt it!" he prompted, answering his own question. Because of a promise he had made to my father some thirty years ago, Gill was to relay a tale that he claimed to have never told before. A story he felt would never be revealed by anyone else, especially my father. An event, that Gill could no longer keep concealed.

The late night Northern saga of suspense held my interest long past midnight. Less than a week later I received another late night phone call, right on twelve o'clock. Gill had promised to call back soon; he could be honing his timing, or possibly..? "Collect call to Jamie from Jimmy," stated the operator.

"Hello there Buds," came the raspy voice. "Thought you would be home and not up to much this time of day, so figured I would give you a call." Late night phone calls from the North never surprised me much and it was a real good time to catch me at home. Realizing that in order to reach a phone the midnight caller had travelled five miles over isolated, snow covered roads, I answered with as cheery a voice as I could muster up. "Glad you called Dad: what have you been up to lately?"

"Steve and I fired up the Six the other day." replied Dad, referring to his buddy the highways grader operator and a six place low wing Cherokee aircraft that sat as a lawn ornament in my Dad's yard for decades. Steve and Dad had been working on getting the Six running when me and my two boys showed up at the Bush Pilot's Roost to share a `Rocky Mountain Owl' Steve was cooking up for the Christmas holiday.

"You guys are not flying around up there are you?" I asked in a slight panic, imagining my father taxiing a bunch of his old cronies around the North country in the aged Six.

"Hell we are," he replied instantly, bringing relief to my taxed mind. "Just got her started up, we got to clear up that little problem in the fuel injection before we'd ever take her off the ground," affirmed the wise old bush pilot.

"Don't you think if the fuel system is not quite up to par, maybe you should have a Certificate of Air Worthiness done on that old plane before you take it air bound, Dad?" I said, wondering what other little problems might show up once the Cherokee was in the air. "Seems to me your next flight may be the last story I get from you," I commented with some concern.

"You don't think for a minute I am stupid enough to get so far away from the highway I couldn't turn'er around and land do you?" asked my dad in a scolding voice. "How in the hell did you think I got as old as I did, by being lucky?" he questioned. "Got to shake the bugs out of her," he continued. "Cheque's cut and setting on a guy's desk in Edmonton. All I got to do is fly the Cherokee over there and pick up the money. That don't sound too difficult does it?"

"Didn't think you would ever sell the old Six," I commented sentimentally, trying to divert this eventual shake down flight of the swift Piper Cherokee.

"Got to," replied Dad. "I need a little cash to rebuild that old cub sitting down at Short's place," he said referring to a broken Super Cub retrieved from the bush strip many midnight moons ago. "Cherokee flies too fast to get into the places I want to go," finished the northern aviator. Stored at a retired flying friend's hangar, located ninety-four miles south on the Alaska highway, dad often talks of fixing up the "Old Savage" and get'er back in the air, where it belongs.

"Can't we talk Bobby into hauling something like that?" I asked. He has his own rig now and must haul down past your place empty now and again," I offered, betting on the generosity of my trucker cousin and the distant chance that Dad would succumb to this safer alternative.

"Hell No!" came the sharp reply. "Now you know I have never had to ship any of my flying equipment by truck yet! And you can bet your hat, this cowboy is not going to start that old bullshit this early on in life. Not by a long shot buddy." Realizing that the northern decision was not going to change, I decided to change the subject, besides, he had made his mind up and that was that. Plans were made for the Savage restoration, nothing would change them now. Trying to get back on the good side of old Pops, I asked in a passive voice. "If you have a few minutes to spare Dad, I have another story to run by you."

"Well if you make'er snappy," he answered. "Everything around here is closed up tighter than a bull's ass in fly time," contributed my father, referring to the absence of night life at the rustic Pink Mountain post office. "We got quite a little storm brewing up here and there is no heat in this here phone booth," he said in a mock complaint about the cold weather.

"What you got?"

GROUNDED

It was a cold blustery winter's afternoon in Fort Nelson. Gill and his pilot buddy Jimmy `Midnight' Anderson were sitting in the Fort Hotel having a beer and Clamato juice. Working the pipeline as a Caterpillar operator, Gill found that partying with Midnight was starting to interfere with his work; so Gill up and quit his dozer job. "It was too damn cold to be riding that iron equipment anyhow," Gill had stated at different times.

Suddenly the bar doors flew open spilling the northern winter inside and drawing the immediate attention of the few bar patrons in the premises. Two uniformed officers stepped through the double-wide doorway as a cold chill filled the hotel bar room. Walking directly over to the table where Gill and his flying friend were seated, the taller of the two asked of Gill's table companion. "Your name Lyle James Anderson?"

"I have been using that name all my life, so I certainly hope it is," replied Gill's buddy. "Who, might I ask, wants to know?".

"Investigation Officers Sayward and Dawson, Department Of Transport, Enforcement Branch. We are serving you, Mr. Anderson, with a summons," stated the large officer.

"As of now we are red-tagging your Piper super cub, identifying letters CF-JST," added his smaller comrade Dawson. "The Compliance Investigative Department perceives you have been flying your craft with makeshift

parts," stated the slightly built officer. "Alleged sightings reported to the local Flight Service Specialists, suggest that you are transporting live caribou with said plane," quoted the investigation officer shaking his head in disbelief.

"There isn't anything wrong with the way the savage flies," replied Jimmy. "Me and the Reverend here had her up in the Snake River country doing a little wildlife count earlier this morning," declared the bush pilot. Ordaining his drinking partner Gill with a nod of his weather beaten cow boy hat) "She was flying fine."

"I'm sorry sir," insisted the smaller officer. "The Compliance Investigative Department was informed that your craft has been repaired in the bush, using willow to support cracked or broken wing struts. Reports to the Department also indicate a damaged wing was repaired with bed sheets in place of aeroplane fabric," stated Dawson. Head shaking in disapproval, the accusation was followed with a merciless voice saying, "Your bush repaired aircraft has been declared unfit for flight Mr. Anderson!"

"The Enforcement Branch has impounded your plane," added officer Sayward, while serving Jimmy the legal paper. "The aircraft is to remain tied down at the Fort Nelson airport until such time as it is released to you through the courts," finished the tall officer. "Technically, your aircraft now belongs to the federal government and is grounded!"

"I'll handle this Jimmy" roared Gill. Jumping up from his bar chair, the big ex-catskinner swung his giant right fist towards the pointed chin of the tall officer. With a movement as quick as a bush cat, the cowboy pilot flashed his hand through the air and caught the wrist of his large friend in mid flight.

"INNKeeper"
MORE BEER

"Hold'er there Buds," exclaimed Jimmy. "These boys are only doing their jobs," he explained to Gill, stepping between the two large men showing mutual disapproval of each other.

"Now let's all sit down and talk this over," soothed Jimmy. "You boys will have to excuse the Reverend Gill here, he gets a little excited every now and again," Jimmy explained with a smile.

"Now why can't we have a beer and work this thing out?" questioned Jimmy. "I fully admit the Jackpine Savage has a few bush rigged parts on her," confessed the backwoods aircraft mechanic. "However if I shut down for D.O.T. inspection, every time the Savage and I had a rough landing, we'd never be in the air," reasoned the recently deplaned pilot.

"We are fully aware of bush flying difficulties in the north Mister Anderson," retorted officer Sayward sternly. "However we must ask for your keys to the Super Cub."

"God damn if you need my keys, here's my keys!" Jimmy exclaimed and slapped them down on the table. "Now, you boys got time for one beer?"

"We have to fly out to Fort St. John, then on to Edmonton, for court in the morning," responded Sayward. "But thank you for the offer."

"If you boys plan on leaving this afternoon, you had better change your minds," countered Jimmy. "I do not like the looks of that storm heading this way. Normally storms that come in from the east or west can be bad enough," he explained. "But every now and again, one will slip out of the Arctic over Fort Simpson and travel down the Liard River valley to freeze things up real tight around here."

"We are aware of the storm moving in sir and are on our way immediately," returned the larger officer. Sayward wanted no more delays, stationed in Edmonton for the past two years he well knew the sudden dangers of Northern winter storms.

"O.K. boys if you gotta go, you gotta go and good luck to you," uttered the disillusioned pilot. The two uniformed men turned in unison and walked out of the hotel; taking with them the keys to Jimmy's livelihood and lifestyle.

"Innkeeper!" Cried Gill knowingly. "More beer!"

"Forget it tonight partner. Let's try to put this behind us," soothed the large friend. "Those boys better not try that flight tonight, there is bad weather coming in; I can feel it in my bones," proclaimed the seasoned skinner with wisdom. "We'll deal with all this government bullshit in the morning Buds," he said, lightly punching Jimmy in the shoulder to punctuate his bar room decision.

Flight schedule a bit behind by that last minute distasteful incident at the hotel, the Baron Beechcraft left Fort Nelson just ahead of the storm that had moved in rather quickly. With no time to sit and wait out weather the two chose to fly Visual Flight Rules, rather than taking time to complete the Instrument Flight Rule clearance.

Travelling south at over two-hundred miles per hour, Sayward knew that the Baron would easily out run the storm. In less than an hour and a half he and Dawson would be set down at the Fort St. John airport, with a hot coffee in their hands. Filing an IFR from there to Edmonton could be done in the time it took to grab a sandwich at the terminal building restaurant. Estimated Time of Arrival in Edmonton would still be well ahead of dusk.

Weather forecast to the south called for cumulus clouds, nice white puffy dome shaped balls of cotton in the blue sky. Miles of air space should separate the condensed mass of water vapour floating in the sky. Child's play to fly around, or he could cloud fly through some of the light stuff, thought Dawson. Sayward wouldn't stand for flying through clouds too thick, but surely he wouldn't object to one or two sparse clouds in this remote area, reasoned the younger pilot.

"Sayward seemed a lot more relaxed," determined Dawson. Tomorrow was Sayward's last official duty for the force. Stressed out from the pressure of his last case Sayward jumped at the invite to accompany Dawson on this routine flight from the north, he needed to get away for awhile. Dawson had insisted that the old hunting partners go on a week long hunting trip around Fort Nelson and return with the grounded Baron in time for the big trial. Bagging a big bull moose on the last morning of the hunt had put the return flight a little behind schedule.

Cumulus congestus clouds were forming on the far horizon. Dawson hoped they were friendly and the towering air masses wouldn't build any higher, or thicker. "Possible icing?" wondered Dawson to himself. It was too late to return to Fort Nelson. Turning at this narrowed point in the valley would be impossible for the twin engine craft. Clouds bunching up ahead were not a problem. They could fly through that easily enough the pilot calculated, or he could skirt around the problem weather.

Brand new, the Baron was a jewel to fly and it was imperative that Sayward be in the Edmonton Supreme Court in the morning. What Dawson was unprepared for was the mass of cumulonimbus looming down the draw of the mountainous valley.

Wedged between the frozen earth and a moisture saturated warm front, the cold Arctic air mass could cause snow or even icing, where the extreme air temperatures clashed. Fully aware that the optional, pneumatic rubber de-icing boots designed for the Beechcraft wing system had not been added to the craft, Dawson pressed on.

The recently purchased four place Beechcraft, added to the Department Of Transport fleet was slated for Fort Nelson via Vancouver. Fully decked out with the newly added D.O.T. red striping, the craft had been flown directly to the northern out post. It was discovered, when the craft landed at the Nelson strip, that the Baron had no optional wing or tail unit de-icing system. Nor would any other de-icing options (except a pilot's storm window) be found on the southern orientated craft.

Immediately grounded, the Beechcraft was to remain parked until this mix-up could be sorted out by the paper mill that travelled amongst the department heads involved. Travelling by domestic flight to Fort Nelson, Dawson and Sayward were to fly the grounded Beechcraft on to Edmonton where the optional icing equipment would be added to the craft for northern flying survival.

Snow scudded from the banks of cumulative clouds above the mountain range and blew stiffly into the Baron's nose. Under gentler circumstances the aircraft would have soared easily above the peaks that lay ahead. Ice forming on the wings leading edges and on the tail assembly had violated the aerodynamics of the Baron's design. Having no choice, Dawson would have to work his way around the storm front.

Known for his slow temper and quiet manner, flying gave Dawson all the thrills he needed. Some of his so called friends indicated that there were times when danger seemed to exhilarate the clean cut bachelor boy. He handled the controls with ease, skirting the transition band cushioning the warm front tumbling over the heavy cold ground air. Landscape ahead was snow covered and wild. On maps, the ranges into which the plane was headed were clearly defined, but from the air, mountains and valleys appeared as one continuous wilderness. At the controls of the Beechcraft, Dawson fought for altitude. After thirty minutes of being thrown around and tossed to and fro in the high winds, he began to doubt his instruments. Although equipped for blind flying the pilot felt the craft was very likely way off course. With the plane bouncing so severely, it was hard to tell.

"Had he turned south?" wondered Dawson. "They should have been above this mess by now." Headings from the list on the envelope in Sayward's hands had been relayed with a grim smile, but Dawson had lost track of the turns. Full tanks of fuel assured him they would eventually out fly this storm.

Mountains looming on either side, Sayward was gazing through the snow shooting into the windshield. His smile tightened. Glancing through the side cockpit window he could make out the shapes of eerie snow covered peaks all around the aircraft. Some were below and some suddenly rose ghostlike out of the cold, wispy mist.

Roaring through crags and valleys, irregular patterns of forced air masses, begetting more winds to clash violently together. Up drafts lifting. Side-drafts buffeting. High winds racing over the uneven northern mountain terrain created invisible turbulence within the massive air current.

Leaned right out the twin two-hundred and sixty hp Continentals were receiving the purest mixture of gasoline and oxygen. Luckily the freshly bagged moose had been quartered, wrapped in a fine cotton mesh meat bag and loaded on a Northern FreightWays truck to Fort St. John to be cut and wrapped, then sent on to Edmonton. A large canvas tent with enough camping gear for a ten day hunt was also shipped by truck. Loaded light with only the men's personal gear and rifles, the Baron was still refusing to climb. Like a bull in a rodeo pen the aircraft bounced, using full energy but not going anywhere. Tossed like a falling leaf in a breeze, the Baron fell into a down-draft.

In still air at sea level, the Baron Beechcraft could climb at a rate of 1,248 ft. per minute. Winds pushing against ice covered wings of the moisture laden plane, caused the craft to lose both altitude and headway. With forward movement stalled and aerodynamics hampered by the icy design change, the plane began to lose vacuum behind the trailing edge of it's wings. Reeds of the stall horn sounded their alarm, filling the cabin with a piercing squeal, warning the occupants the aircraft was dangerously close to tumbling out of control.

"Should those things be going off," asked Sayward with the tight smile still on his face.

"Back pressure from the mountains," lied Dawson to his copilot who was fully aware of the danger involved. "Doesn't mean a thing." Looking at his companion for affirmation Dawson said, "might nose her down to build up some air speed. Once we have speed built up, breaking regulation or not, we will have to switch from VFR to IFR and blast ourselves up through that storm," finished Dawson.

"Go for it," encouraged Sayward. There was no oxygen system on board and although Sayward found cloud flying distasteful, he wanted the Baron high above the flurries and around those snow clouds. "Even without oxygen on board whatever they had to deal with up there couldn't possibly be any worse than this," reasoned the seasoned copilot. "Could it?"

"I'm going into the canyon," Dawson said to no one in particular. Twisting through a cloud opening and exposing a valley far below Dawson flew the Baron between two mountains towards the lower land. Rushing towards the distant valley floor the stall horns were starting to fade as the airspeed grew. Suddenly sheets of ice crystal were plastering the front windshield.

Disregarding the heated air flow from the fifty-thousand BTU Janitrol blowing through the windscreen defrosting vents, the frozen raindrops adhered to the craft glass. The craft did not have optional alcohol de-icing for port side. Falling from the high warm front, rain drops touching the frozen surface of the plane were instantly turning into fine sheets of ice.

Instrument panel flood lights, desperately displaying the cockpit dials and gauges, were glowing through ice covered cab windows, illuminating a cold deathly sheen, reflecting from the ice laden wings.

"Pull'er up!" hollered Sayward, the grim smile no longer on his face..

"It won't come up," shouted Dawson over the roar of the craft being pushed and pulled through the eye of the storm. "Getting heavy; too much weight on the wings." Thud, thud, ice flying from the props was slamming into the metal cabin.

"Prop icing up," stated Sayward. "Starboard engine losing rpm."

"Sergeant send a Mayday," commanded the pilot, "according to the altimeter were going down!" He could see nothing through the snow.

Where could they set the craft down safely? Over two thousand feet of runway would be needed to land the Baron Beechcraft. Where was he going to find a place like that in this country in the middle of a snow storm? The plane broke through the shifting clouds for a moments view of the land and then a sliver of white shone up through the mass of darkened tree tops.

"A river," shouted Sayward, pointing down. Fighting ice build up and frozen in place ailerons, Dawson was directing the falling aeroplane towards the longest straight stretch of visible river.

"Mayday, Mayday," came the faint reception fading in and out over the radio speaker of the sleek low winged metal American aircraft as it was landing at the Fort Nelson airport.

"Mayday, icing up, losing altitude, an hour and fifteen minutes in route; Fort Nelson — Fort St. John. Going down for a landing on a short stretch of river, large cut bank on the south side," crackle crackle.

BACK AT THE FORT

"Jimmy, you have got to come to the lobby," exclaimed an excited hotel desk clerk as she came rushing into the bar room. "An American couple that are getting a room said that when they were landing at the airport about an hour ago they heard a Mayday. Could it be from the two guys that confiscated your plane?" she questioned.

"What's that dear, a Mayday? Bring them on in here," proclaimed Jimmy! "Grab them a beer and put it on my tab."

"You put that one on my tab honey!" countered Jimmy's sidekick Gill.

"Yes we heard the Mayday just as we were coming in," revealed the young woman. "The weather was so bad, it almost forced us down."

"We were sure glad to find the airstrip," the young man added. "My wife and I are flying down from Fairbanks to Seattle. This weather came up behind us from the north west and we barely managed to outrun the snow and wind. I guess we were a lot more fortunate than those poor souls that crashed out there somewhere," surmised the young pilot.

"When that old wind comes down the Liard River, it can get cold. What all was said as they were going down?" queried Jimmy.

"What we were picking up from the broken transmission was indicating that an hour of their flight plan from Fort Nelson to Fort St. John had been completed," the American pilot relayed to Jimmy. "They were also indicating that an emergency river landing was in progress. Apparently there is a large cut bank on the south side of the river. The Department of Transport assured us that a search would be initiated out of Fort St. John at daylight," contributed the young pilot. "They must have run into a transition between a warm south front climbing over that arctic cold air mass," he added. "Freezing rain probably caused everything to ice-up."

"They said, it would be suicide to send someone out tonight," confirmed his spouse. "The search would have to wait till morning and this weather to pass over," she added.

"If those boys are hurt at all, they will never last till morning," alleged Anderson with concern. "It still could drop down to 40 below tonight and that storm could go on for days."

"Jimmy, there is nothing you can do for them " Gill said with determination.

"Could be a break in the weather after this little storm has blown itself out, Reverend." Thoughtfully Jimmy reflected on the Mayday. "I have been trying to place where those fellows went down. High head winds must have turned them fellows around," declared Jimmy to Gill. "That stretch of river bank they mentioned in the Mayday is located on the north side of the river." Jimmy said with quiet decision. "Not the south side! And the Sikanni Chief is the only river with banks that high," he said with conviction. "I'd bet my hat on that one!"

"Jimmy," observed Gill in desperation. "Even if you could pinpoint where those unfortunate souls went down, you don't have a plane to fly in. It's confiscated!" raising his boisterous voice Gill stated, "none of this is your problem Jimmy!"

Gill was finding Jimmy's behaviour a little worrying. Understandably he was a bit upset over the loss of his Savage. That kind of worry could kill a good time. Fact is this morning started out real fine, with an early fly around. Bad weather brewing on the distant horizon had shortened the Fontas country bound trip, in favour of a more civil surrounding. No argument from Gill, he was quite comfortable sitting in the back of the two seat cub viewing the expanse of the northern wilderness high in the air, rather than from the hard seat of a cold old bush cat. Jimmy had indicated to Gill in his good natured way that when the Northern winds hit the Nelson area the Jackpine Savage would just as soon be tied down on the strip. Since the Mayday however, Jimmy seemed to have forgotten about his flying machine. He spoke only of the downed aircraft's location.

Gill had honest concern for the plight of the two Department officers who had confiscated his partner's plane earlier. It bothered Gill a little when visualizingthe isolated crash site of the downed aircraft and crew. Come to think about it, things had gotten real depressing ever since those government air jockeys had arrived and ruined his liquid lunch. First one today for Jimmy and him too! But there was no way anyone was going to find those poor unfortunate souls tonight.

"Hell they should know where they are," justified Gill. "They're the ones that are down out there.!" Throwing his arm around his buddy's shoulder, Gill proceeded to steer Jimmy towards the bar. "What his Buds was needing right now was another drink. "Got to get his mind off of this depressing scenario," thought Gill. "Jimmy you have to forget those guys tonight, now tell me, is it really true that you once landed the Savage in a Safeway parking lot because you had run out of cigarettes? Ha ha, come on old partner tell me what the clerk said, ha ha."

"Listen buds; morning could be too late for those two fellows," said Jimmy interrupting Gill's logical concept and continuing on in a sobering voice, he said to his big hearted pal, "those boys might not make it through the night!"

"Jimmy you don't even have your keys to the aeroplane!" pointed out Gill in exasperation. "Government will look after their boys in the morning," confirmed the big cat skinner. "Forget it partner: let's grab a fresh beer."

"I was just outside Buds and the ceiling is starting to lift; I could see light patches to the north," Jimmy stated with a low excitement creeping into his voice. "The weather is starting to shift buds: and don't you ever think this cowboy cannot start the Savage without a key," said the bush pilot with a 'devil may care' twinkle in his eye. For the first time since hearing of the Mayday earlier, Gill saw the old mischievous smile again tugging at the corner of his flying friend's mouth.

"What can we do, Jimmy?" said Gill; resigned, giving up on trying to divert Jimmy from this mission of disaster.

"You got your car handy, Reverend?"

Driving east along the seven miles of snow covered road that lay between Fort Nelson and it's flight strip Gill could see that indeed the storm was letting up. However, dropping to thirty below, the temperature had become colder and as the cloud cover was dissipating the temperature would drop even more.

With a taste of the special brew brought along for this occasion Gill was listening to the plan Jimmy had devised. The brew was certainly up to par. Made under the careful instructions of Jimmy, the Innkeeper (as Gill liked to call his buddy behind the bar) had poured the concoction of hot water, cinnamon, butter and brown sugar into Gill's unbreakable steel thermos bottle. Topping the ingredients off with Bacardi's dark rum Gill assured Jimmy that even if it was dropped from an aeroplane, his creation would be safe. This bottle, momentarily forgotten after a brief coffee break, had been crush tested under the track of the very D-8 caterpillar Gill used to skin. A little hard to dig out of the frozen muskeg with his track shovel afterwards, but it didn't even get scratched, and the coffee was still hot.

"O.K. Buds, this is it," said the cowboy passenger, "turn your interior light off and slow down a little, we do not want this little excursion to end right here," cautioned Jimmy. Twisting the empty steel cup back on the unbreakable bottle he tossed it out the slight opening of the car door. Following the thermos of brew, the grounded cowboy was rolling out of the slow moving vehicle and into the ditch of the narrow road that ran parallel to the runway. Picking up speed, with passenger door ajar, Gill drove away into the night.

Scrambling across the ditch, the thermos wedged securely against his side with elbow and forearm, Jimmy spotted the Savage where he had left it. Across the open field slinking from bush to bush, like a troubled coyote he trotted the snow covered two-hundred yards in a few minutes.

The guarded cowboy, stopping and looking both ways, stood upright and casually started walking towards his seized aeroplane. Releasing the tie-downs and lifting the engine cowlings he reached inside. After 'jimmying' the wires of the Savage and latching the engine cowling, he climbed inside and hit the starter button. Cough, cough, sputter. Was it the cold weather? Or had those government sky jockeys been mucking with his plane? "Chug, Varrrooooomm" the Savage came to life.

Jimmy slid the throttle slowly forward and hoping the guy in the tower was down stairs for a coffee, he directed the Savage towards the strip. Whirls of snow flying in it's wake, the Piper Super Cub taxied over to # 25 and within moments the Jackpine Savage was cruising down the snow covered runway. After a leisurely warm up ski and ample ground speed the light craft lifted off like a large bird of prey into the night sky. Flying low and riding the diminishing tail winds of the storm he was guiding the liberated Savage southeast towards where he sensed the D.O.T. plane had gone down.

SURVIVAL

Upon landing Sayward had been knocked unconscious and received a large gash across his right temple from being whipped into the windshield of the Beechcraft Baron. Dawson was concerned about his friends semiconscious condition and loss of blood. Too frigid to speak, the Corporal carefully reached over and shook the snow from the shoulders of his injured friend, who was again drifting off into a motionless sleep.

Wrenching pain from a broken hand shot up his arm, hours of extreme cold was numbing most feelings flowing from the fracture, sometimes he was able to forget; immediately the set down flashed to his mind. What could he have done different to keep the plane in the air? What's to happen now?

Being the senior pilot, Dawson had control of the twin engine craft when the electrically retractable tricycle gear, unfolded from the under wing and snapped in to place. Bright green landing indicator lights on the dash verified this operation had been completed.

"Ice must have adhered to the landing gear cowling," mused the downed pilot. "Crushed ice must have activated the landing gear lights, while preventing the port side wheeled unit from locking into place."

Dawson felt the port landing gear collapsing soon after the Cleveland wheels of the craft touched down on the frozen emergency strip. Landing speed was slowed dramatically by the snow blanket covering the frozen runway and the Baron could not lift for a second try. Belly deep in snow, the ice laden Beechcraft was committed to the river landing.

Veering left; the port wing section of the cantilever low-wing monoplane connecting with a small clump of buck brush had swung the landing craft off track. The starboard wing spun the craft around ninety degrees and the Baron flew into the edge of the frozen water way. Ice and river rock sprayed against the metal alloy skin of the Beechcraft when the six foot six inch Hartzell two-blade propeller dug into the river's winter bed. Emitting a shudder from the two-hundred and sixty hp Continental flat-six engine, the Baron ploughed nose first to a halt. Dawson's thumb was ripped from its socket as his right hand travelled beyond the aircraft's column steering control which he had tightly clutched in his hands.

Dazed and reeling with pain, Dawson was thankful to be conscious and alive. Fortunately the deep snow slowed the Baron considerably before the crash. His copilot was not so lucky. At a glance Dawson saw blood both on the corner of the windshield and also seeping from the hair line of the copilot's right temple.

From habit Dawson, with his right hand, quickly reached for the dash mounted toggle switches to shut down the engines. Searing pain shooting from the busted thumb demanded he use his left hand to kill the fifty amp alternator charging the half dozen spark plugs that kept the one-hundred and ninety-four kilowatt starboard engine rotating. Unharmed by the emergency landing, the right engine was supported high above the gravel shore by a tripod configuration of the nose, left wing and the intact starboard landing strut. For safety reasons Dawson also switched off the twenty-four volt circuit that continued to feed the friction stalled port engine. Aviation fuel vapours permeating the interior of the damaged craft convinced the aviator to seek a less explosive site and he began evacuating the protecting cockpit of the beached Baron without delay.

Slumping forward in the copilot's seat, Sayward was held in place by the quick acting inertia reel equipped shoulder harness. Standard on all four cab seats, Sayward would have fallen over the pilot, without the restraint of the single diagonal strap. The sheer dead weight of the huge man would have pinned Dawson in the cabin of the plane.

Sticking his mangled gloved hand into the front of his fleece lined flight jacket, Dawson reached around behind the pilot's seat with his left arm and levered himself through the small space between the two front seats. Once in the rear seat, he unlocked and booted the emergency window exit from the starboard side of the busted Baron's fuselage. Climbing out through the exit, Dawson stood on the slightly tilted right wing. With his left hand he opened the front passenger cockpit door and reached across to unbuckle Sayward's shoulder harness.

Removing his still breathing unconscious friend from the tilted cockpit was difficult. Fortunately his wounded copilot started to come around. "There seems to be something running into my eyes Corporal, am I bleeding?" Sayward was starting to come around, but still somewhat disoriented, Sayward had not called him Corporal for

"MAYDAY"

years. Helping Sayward slowly climb through the three foot square opening of the cabin door. Dawson carefully assisted his injured ex-sergeant from the elevated wing of the damaged craft down to the ground.

Staff Sergeant Sayward was the corporal's commanding officer in the R.C.M.P.. Finishing his tour with the forces five years sooner than Sergeant Sayward had, Corporal Dawson was the main influence in his former sergeant's decision to leave a comfortable retirement and start another career. Both were now members of the Department Of Transport's, Enforcement Branch. Tomorrow's court case in Edmonton was to be the last of Sayward's official R. C. M. P. duties.

Reflecting the still images of two blanket wrapped forms, a small fire was lamely trying to survive the coldness of the night. Emergency blankets, closely draping over huddled shoulders, did little to stop cold from penetrating vital organs of the exposed men. Dry winter grass and wood found under a large tree lying discarded along the frozen river bank had been used to build the fire. Left unattended the source of life giving heat was dying in the darkening campsite. Ice beads forming on Officer Dawson's eyelashes became heavy, as he vainly fought the urge to doze off into eternal sleep.

"Crack!" snapped a coal into the mesmerising slumber of the cold silence. Dawson, glancing at the fire from where the noise of the protesting ember originated, realized in a panic the survival fire was almost dead. Dawson's life depended on that fire, if it went out they had no more tinder to relight it. Small wood was getting scarce, soon there would be only large wood left in the brush pile at the base of the tree he had been salvaging fuel from. Wood left in the pile was too large to be ignited by the heat of the dying fire.

Carefully Dawson placed the last of the dead twigs on the pitiful blaze and in a moment it died to a flicker, the life heat of fire momentarily whisked away by the cold fuel. Dawson slowly built the flame until grudgingly the reflecting light bounced back from the coarsely barked stump of the nature fallen tree. That was too close! With no fire they would surely perish. Retired ex-R.C.M.P. Staff Sergeant Sayward slowly opened his eyes and shook his aching blood soaked head. "I will be all right Corporal," came the hoarse voice. Although the firelight reflecting in his eyes showed sincerity, Dawson did not believe him for a moment. Enforcement Officer Dawson was beginning to fear for his friend's life.

Dawson very softly woke his older friend, moving the big man's head in the slightest would reopen his ex-Sergeant's seeping wound, "Just resting my eyes Corporal," responded the wounded officer bravely. .

"It does not seem as bad now Sergeant." Corporal Dawson said in a calming voice. Looking at the blood seeping down across Sayward's face from the forehead wound Dawson noticed the whiteness of freezing skin framing the wound. It was hard to convince himself that Sayward was not losing too much oxygen carrying blood. Why did he keep waking his long time friend? Both would be frozen stiff by morning anyway. Was it fear of being left alone with death in the cold dark?

Brushing fresh fallen snow clumsily from his partner's shoulders and then huddling close to the cold body of his Sergeant, he waited. Slowly he felt his eyes closing. Wait, just wait, he was so tired; he was ready for the eternal peace of cold sleep, no more pain. Ice covered eye lashes gently laid to rest on the frozen cheek tissue. Just wait , no more pain. Floating, just relax, don't fight it, feel heat from the cold, Dawson was still, it's so quiet; his wandering mind travelling back to the carefree days of his youth.

First flight solo in a Piper cub J-3. It was a hot sunny day. Rays of sunlight flickered through the tall trees border lining the dirt strip he was about to try his first solo landing. Life was grand! "How am I doing, Norm?" he remembered yelling back over his shoulder in mock pretence. The grizzled instructor would not be on the back controls today if something went faulty. Faintly, some where in the back ground of this memory that was cheating the dreariness of death, the purring sound of the training crafts motor. .

Over there! Light from the sun's rays was slicing through the forest. Dawson could almost feel the scorching heat of the hot day. The sunlight seemed to follow the river; light flashing through the trees here and there. Dawson had heard of these phenomenon before, a light from the sky would cover their frozen bodies just before the end. There it was again, coming towards him and his doomed friend. It would be over soon. Still the engine sound, the J-3 seemed closer. Was he going to leave this life insane? Or was he in his Piper trainer? It all seemed so real. Dropping from the sky the heavenly light was still following the river. An aeroplane? Not in this storm!" Dawson assured himself. "Wait, was that engine noise again?"

"It was an aeroplane!" Excitement tugging at his heart Dawson sat watching the light aircraft wing by thirty feet above the snow covered river runway. "Of course the Cub could not land with the Baron lying sideways across the river, there was not enough clear runway," he reasoned. Struggling to his numbed feet Dawson felt the slivers of frost bite knifing up his legs. Peering after the plane, he was

Eagle Landing
Singer © 95.

wondering. "Where did that silhouetted Cub come from? Did the pilot see the small signal fire? If he reports our location, perhaps we will be rescued by morning." Turning back to the fire he wanted to share the new development with his friend. Slouched forward, Sayward had not seen the craft, he was unconscious again.

"Who was he kidding? Sayward would not see tomorrow, he had lost too much blood. Hell! Nobody is going to make it through the night!" The last of the usable firewood was now a bed of coals supporting a few flickering flames. Neither his broken hand or his feet had any feeling. "No more strength left; just sit with Sayward," he thought. "Hold him up straight, he would not like to be found hunched over like that, Sayward was a proud man." Turning his back on the diminishing landing light of the rescue Cub, Dawson gently sat his friend upright and sitting along side put Sayward's left arm over his shoulder. There was little heat to be salvaged from the large man's cold body, but this way if Dawson fell asleep before morning his friend would still be sitting upright when the pair were found.

Now where were we? Oh yes the warm sound of the Piper trainer; in the background fading, fading away, going for rescue. Only a few more hours until daybreak; it will be warmer then. They would be able to see beyond the campfire flicker. Everything would be all right in the morning light.

Snuggling next to his near frozen friend, he listened to the small craft motor fading into the distance. "God it was cold!" Then the engine noise quit. "What happened to our rescue plane? Was its pilot to freeze in this cold also?" Then, lights in the trees again, this time it was shining through the scrub willow that grew along the shifting banks of the meandering river bed.

FEATHERING OUT

Easing the stick back between his legs and silently dropping out of the sky like a swooping bird 'Midnight' with landing flaps of the Savage full on, set down on the short landing strip. The river snow was crystallized and the Savage sank belly deep into the deep powder, quickly slowing the Piper Cub.

Sliding the throttle forward, the Cub's Lycoming motor picked up rpm, lifting the snow covered skis slightly as the Jackpine Savage skied by the two stranded men and circled around the Baron. Coming to a large bend in the river, the cub skied a large circle and returned back to the set trail circling the Baron. Taxiing along in it's own set ski tracks the Savage came to rest a few yards from the men crouching amidst the river's collection of driftwood. Seeing the still blankets huddled around the fire when he first flew by, Jimmy was relieved to see the one fellow now getting up. "Hope I'm not too late for the other," thought Midnight.

Seeing the second blanket move as he shut down the 150 HP Lycoming engine a smile crossed his face. Flopping open the cub door and jumping down from the plane, the cowboy pilot began ploughing through snow that was tugging at his knees, as he broke trail to the men struggling to get up. In greeting the two Enforcement Officers, who had just grounded him some hours before, Jimmy said, "now what are you two boys up to the way and hell and gone out here?"

Offering a hand to the tall man with the bloody head wound, Jimmy helped him to his feet and upon inspecting both men for injury, he started wading back along the crystal snow covered trail to the Cub. Returning with a small towel used for wiping the wind shield on foggy nights, Jimmy proceeded to place the clean soft rag over the cold bleeding wound of the tall Sergeant.

Magically, a warm cup was being placed in the Corporal's left hand. Warmth of the steel cup was seeping through Dawson's light leather flying glove, the heat source was heaven. Touching the warm nectar to frost bitten lips, the bush pilot's brew was the most delicious drink he had ever tasted. His stressed body immediately relaxed. Holding the cup to Sayward's lips, his partner inhaled the mysterious warm fumes radiating from the steel container. Walking over to the dying fire and taking large diameter pieces of drift wood, the cowboy stacked them in a tepee style pile, against the base of the large old tree root. The small flamed fire faintly flickered nearby.

"Does he think that small flame is going to ignite those huge hunks of drift wood?" absently wondered Dawson, his ice laden lashes trying to freeze together across glazed eyes that methodically followed the bush pilot returning to the super cub. Turning his attention back to his injured friend, Dawson could not keep the small cup of the bush pilot's brew to Sayward's lips. His long time friend was now starting to shake violently, rescue was to be too late for Sayward. Shelter in the Cub would not help, there would still be no real heat. Hypothermia would take Sayward soon! He needed heat now.

Sayward and he had some good times together, but Sayward was dying. "Damn that storm!" he cried out to the cold dark sky; only to be answered by silence.

Moments later the cowboy returned carrying a steel thermos in his right hand and what looked like a blue tobacco can in his left. Dawson savoured the idea of another swig or two from the thermos which obviously held the same brew as the metal cup held in his hands, but as for a smoke? He was too cold to smoke, he was too cold for anything, he glanced towards the dying flames; would the cowboy have an axe? Didn't matter it would take a while for the fire to grow, it was too late for Sayward, he was starting to shiver real deep. Maybe the heat of the thermos's brew will warm him? If Sayward would just stop shaking so hard then Dawson could get some of the warm brew inside his partner.

"You boys step over here a minute," the cowboy pilot said to Dawson, beckoning with a nod of his head. Gently guiding his partner, Dawson stepped to the outer edge of the campsite. Steel thermos set in the snow, the cowboy pilot was stepping past the men and moving closer to the stack of drift wood, while removing the lid from the Player's tobacco tin. Dawson's nostril's were assaulted as the cowboy passed by him. "That smell! It had driven them from the shelter of the Baron," thought Dawson.

"Watch yourself there buds," cautioned the bush pilot, "we're going to make Cowboy Fire! Backwoods style."

"That was not tobacco in that blue tin can," realized Dawson. "It was full of high octane aviation gas!" Splashing off the large lengths of driftwood that were lying against the large root, the over spray from the gas was entering the small campfire's domain.

"Whoosh," responded the instant ball of fire to the gas drenched pile of brush. Bursting into flames and launching an inferno of heat racing along the uprooted gnarled tree root, the "cowboy fire" was torching up the black Northern night sky. Intense heat flaring from the burst of combustion started water flowing down Dawson's face. Was it ice leaving his frozen eyelashes, or tears of gratitude for this life giving heat. Stepping quickly away from the scorching heat, the cowboy retrieving the thermos from the snow began pouring another shot of brew in the now empty steel cup.

"You fellows got to be about the hardest bunch to slow down for a drink, I have ever come across!" claimed the cowboy bush pilot. Dawson was noticing the intense heat from the gas assisted fire was already slowing the shivering of Sayward considerably. A slight smile was warming the tall Sergeant's battered face.

Suddenly the reflecting emergency blankets were obstructing the fire's radiating heat. Removing his friend's blanket, Dawson slowly started turning Sayward as if roasting a large fish near a too hot fire. After a time of watching the injured pair perform, the cowboy pilot decided they would be all right and walked over to the Cub. Firing up the engine and skiing along in the tracks set by the Super Cub while landing; the Savage headed up river. By the time Dawson saw the lights of the Savage disappear he and Sayward, were taking off their heavy flight jackets and hanging them from a root. Heat could now penetrate the wool plaid shirts of the men and warm the light Stanfields covering the frozen skin of the two men.

Returning from setting a trail up river, Jimmy was skiing by the well lit camp, he could see things were moving around a bit better. Turning the Savage around in the down stream cul-de-sac and scooting around the obstructing tail of the Baron, he was pulling up to the trail leading to the diminishing cow boy fire. Walking along the beaten trail from the plane to the campfire Jimmy was offered a drink by the smiling officers as soon as he entered the circle of comforting heat. Checking out the crew he noticed a bit more colour in Sayward's face. Dawson's hand still hung, of course, useless at his side.

Using a stick put off to the side earlier, he pushed the charred driftwood ends further into the fire. Flames generated from the added fuel vainly tried to reach the glazed embers of the charred root cavity that thirty minutes ago were glowing a radiant red. Now darkened the embers did little to reflect the heat of the remaining wood. Flexible now that the cold had been driven from his bones Dawson put on his own coat but needed Jimmy's help to return Sayward's flight jacket to his slumped shoulders. Sayward had quit shivering noted Dawson, but was having periods of incoherence.

With every thing going as well as expected at the survival camp, Jimmy turned to Dawson and said, "The Savage and I will go beat down a better trail. When I get back that fire will be low and there is no more wood." Dawson could see that! "So you guys be ready to go. The ski trail should be set enough by then to pack all of our weight without breaking through too bad," stated the bush pilot. "Might be a bit bumpy the first trip or two but once the run is smoothed out, she'll be like flying off of the highway," he said with an encouraging smile.

Emergency blankets went back over their shoulders soon after the cub disappeared around the river bend. It was becoming chilly again now that the 'Cowboy Fire' had died down. Darkness and cold began to creep towards the diminishing camp fire.

Twenty minutes later the landing light of the speeding Super Cub shone strongly through the wild shrubbery lining the river bank. Skiing by the two men who were huddling around the small fire Jimmy, completing the turn beyond the defunct Baron for the third time, returned to where the trail headed up to the fire. Abandoning the dying fire, the men were watching the Savage pulling up to the well beaten snow trail. As soon as the prop quit turning, the two, carrying their gear and the thermos, began to trek down the trail to where the Cub stood waiting.

"Climb on into the Savage there out of the weather," Jimmy said straightening the interior of the cub while getting out. "Dawson, you're smallest, you crawl in first and sit on that metal freight bar in the back that stretches across the fuselage. And don't you worry none about Caribou dung, Buds. I cleaned 'er out myself before I came; watch your hand there," cautioned Jimmy with a smile. "You crawl up and sit on the freight board," he said to Sayward pointing to a plywood flooring. "Cross legged would be the most comfortable." Climbing into the pilot's seat he turned to the D.O.T. officers. "Now that I have a captive audience," Jimmy said with a grin. "We have some decisions to make. Seeing as you fellows technically possess the Savage at this time, I want you to be in on the choices."

"What choices Jimmy?" questioned Dawson. They were rescued, what choices could there be now? They had been taxiing up the frozen river for about fifteen minutes until they came to an area wide enough on the crooked river to turn around. Jimmy following the preset tracks made a large circle, turning the Savage back in the direction of the Beechcraft sitting a couple twisting miles down stream. "Can we not just fly out?" Dawson asked.

43

"That is a bit of a problem," replied Jimmy. "I could land with this much weight in the Savage. Taking off now that is a little different. I could pick up in no time with one on board and be in the air heading for Nelson. Two?" grimaced the pilot, "that's a different story. With that broken Beechcraft cluttering up the runway, take off will be a little tight," explained Jimmy. "You boys might have picked a longer strip, you know," he said smiling. "Fact is, if you had not built that snow bank up in front of the plane, I think you would have flown right in to that cut bank, and you fellows probably would still have been sitting in it! Know what I mean?"

Dawson knew what he meant. River curves were at each end of the hastily picked strip. The Baron's grounded airframe had spun around on the ice. Torn, but still attached, the tail section stretched out from the south river bank, blocking the last half of the river strip that the Baron had attempted to land on.

"If we can't fly the two of you out at once we all have to stay," decided Jimmy. "Makes no sense leaving one of you here alone; in case the weather gets bad again and I can't get back for another flight? That would leave one of you here by yourselves with no fire," commented Jimmy, "for only God knows, how long?"

"Makes sense," replied Dawson. The idea of leaving one person alone on the ice in the freezing cold did not appeal much to him either.

"We could sit here and wait for morning. There is a good chance we would be found by tomorrow night," said Jimmy.

"Unless of course another storm comes through," Dawson added. "Or the search is confused by my last radio message."

"The Reverend's thermos is going to run out of liquid, about the same time as your partner here," said the bush pilot. The grin was no longer on his face.

"What can we do, Jimmy?" asked Dawson. By the pasty colour of Sayward's face, Dawson knew that his friend needed help real bad.

"First off we got to beat down that ski track more," said Jimmy as he slowly slid the throttle forward. After some time roaring the cub back and forth on the river runway the two tracks on the snow were wide well-worn strips of icy crystallized snow. "I'm going to make another pass," hollered Jimmy. "We'll wear'er down even smoother and burn a bit more weight out of that left wing tank. Make'er as light as possible, we are going to need all the takeoff speed we can muster up when we round the corner of the river. The Savage must get high enough to nip over the top of that busted Baron tail," expounded the cowboy pilot, "and we only get one try at'er."

Looking out his side window Dawson fully understood the problem. He could see the broken D.O.T. plane. It was pointed nose first into the middle of the frozen snow bank having been pushed up at landing. Tracking the strip past the old camp just before reaching the Baron the Cub had to veer off to the right to get around the broken craft. Building up takeoff speed they would be heading towards the grounded Beechcraft at such speed, that the small craft would not readily steer around the tail of the busted plane. If the Piper Cub did not fly over the tail section that extended into the air, the Cub would become part of the departed Baron. Dawson found himself wondering how the bush pilot could calculate the risk between reducing the weight by burning off fuel and keeping enough fuel to return to the airstrip. Suddenly the prop was silent. Jimmy opening the

45

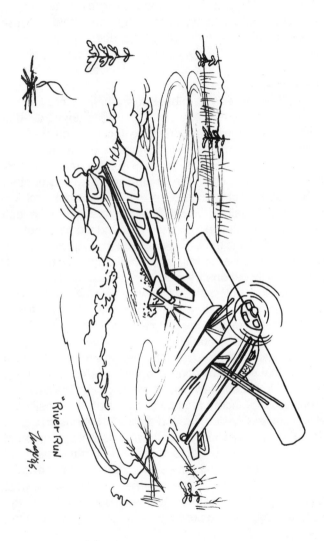

"River Run

door of the Cub and hopping out on to the snow, extended his hand to the still disorientated Sayward. "Yump, out of there partner and let's walk around and work up the circulation for a bit."

"You fellows want to make yellow snow? Now is a good time," said the cowboy with a forced grin. "We want to get rid of as much weight as possible for the takeoff. Once we get in the air there are no facilities. That tail wind that got me down here in damn short time, is going to be bucking us all the way back."

Then taking the empty thermos and walking over to the tail section of the Baron, Jimmy reaching up to where the rudder joined the tail fin, jammed Reverend Gill's thermos bottle solidly into the hinged fitting.

If Jimmy was leaving his friend's expensive thermos stuck on the tail rudder, Dawson figured he must be serious about relieving the plane of as much weight as possible. He was now wishing he had not put on that extra ten pounds since leaving the Mounties.

Cub doors closing for the final time, the Super Cub taxied up river around the left hand bend and skied freely up the narrow crooked river. Two miles up from the river bend, Jimmy made a one-hundred and eighty degree turn and began travelling down stream towards the resting Baron. Around the next river bend the deep soft snow that had ripped parts from the under carriage of the Baron was now a solidly packed ski trail. Stopping on the well beaten path, the pilot checked on his passengers, "You boys all right?" he asked.

With a forced grin Dawson gave a thumbs up sign rather than try to holler an answer over the roar of the prop wash, that was flowing from the front of the aircraft. The Sergeant was nodding off again.

"Leave him sleep," said the Savage pilot knowingly. "As long as he is passed out, he will not move around. We will use his weight as ballast. Looking at the corporal straight in the eye the bush pilot said. "Here is what I want you to do."

RIVER RUNWAY

Hunched over the right side of the limp body of his partner, with right hand safely tucked away inside his tunic, Dawson's left hand was tightly clamped to the steel tubing of the pilot's seat. Leaning forward as far as possible, he squeezed between his friend and the right side of the fuselage, distributing his weight to the front and right of the cab. The plane roared towards the right hand curve of the river. Immediately the light tail-dragger wheel lifted. Like an eight-track auto rewinding repeatedly in his mind, Dawson remembered Jimmy's comments.

"If we don't flip on the corner, once we level out again, centre your weight and stay there no matter what. We will only have one try at this. If we miss I can't stop the Savage before she crashes into your craft."

Rounding the river bend on two skis, with tail in the air, Dawson was amazed at the speed they had achieved. Immediately he shifted his weight to centre over the now snoring carcass of his large friend.

Throttle slammed forward, the engine speed raced as pistons of the large air cooled engine sucked the thirty below air through the intake manifold. Nature cooled compressed air, mixed with the refined aviation gas trapped inside the hot piston chamber's, ignited. Implosive power driving the crank shaft was propelling the bush pitched prop as it was carving it's way through the thick winter air. The

Jackpine Savage leaping to life, went ripping down the winter strip towards the beached Baron. The white form of the lifeless D.O.T. aircraft jutted out across the ice from the south side of the frozen river bank.

In his crouched position Dawson could see the downed craft looming closer. "Wait!" We can not take off yet," screamed his thoughts. He could hardly make out the tail section. The off-white craft blended in with the snow covered bank and whiteness of the frozen flight strip. It was hard to tell where or how high the tail section was. At this angle Dawson could not make out the red identifying strips the department used on their government craft. Speed compressed air gathered under the wing span and the Jackpine Savage lifted off the ice with the labouring prop now clawing for air speed.

"We are not high enough to clear the wreckage!" panicked Dawson, "I cannot make out the tail section." There, a glint from Reverend Gill's thermos reflecting from the landing lights. "The left wing," Dawson's mind screamed, "it's about to clip the thermos." Landing flaps were thrown full on and the Savage catapulted by the redirected cold air flow leaped through the air, gaining immediate altitude; moments before the seemingly inevitable crash, the Savage banked sharply to starboard, allowing the left wing tip to skim over the Baron's tail piece. Flaps flashing back into the wing foil and the plane instantly picked up air speed lost from the sudden change in elevation.

To Dawson's horror the Cub was now heading into the high cut-bank marking the north side of the river. Quickly dropping its left wing, the Jackpine Savage now started banking down stream and levelled out over the river cul-de-sac. Following the frozen waterway for a short distance just above the scrub Jackpine forest, the Savage, with more than adequate airspeed, tilted up for a steady climb into the clear, moonlit, night sky.

Salvaged from the torturing cold, Dawson, while stargazing, gently shook his friend awake. "It's all right we are going to make it!" Sayward nodded his head and was smiling. "His buds understood. The Sergeant was going to be `OKAY'. It was great to be alive!"

Noticing his two fledglings were feeling a bit better, Jimmy turned and lighting up a smoke, said with a smile. "We will have to make sure old Gill gets his thermos back when that plane gets cleaned up."

"Don't worry Jimmy," said Corporal Dawson with conviction, "we will make sure the thermos gets back to Reverend Gill." Smiling faintly, the large sergeant nodded his blood stained head in agreement. Waking his friend occasionally, Dawson noticed each time that Sayward seemed more aware. The stars looked so close you could pluck them from the sky.

"Coco-Fox-trot, JST. Nelson tower," called Jimmy.

"Fort Nelson Tower, JST," came the answer.

"Nelson Tower, request Fort Nelson Ambulance be on hand when I land in half an hour or so," requested Jimmy.

"Will do Mr. Anderson, is everyone all right?"

"Got both of them with me right now. You can deactivate Search and Rescue," smiled the pilot into the radio mike.

Not only by ambulance, was the Jackpine Savage met, but also by R.C.M.P. and D.O.T. officials. Surrounding the Savage, doors were popped open and the two weathered men were gently pulled out of the plane and put into the emergency vehicle.

Walking over to the D.O.T. Department Head who was watching over the care of the Enforcement officers, Jimmy said. "I guess you'll be wanting the Cub back again?"

"We have been trying to ground you Jimmy, at quite an expense I might add, for some time now," replied the Flight Service Station Manager, as he looked the bush pilot in the eye. Taking Jimmy aside he added, "we are truly thankful you brought in our two officers though, and no doubt you realise this is a little embarrassing for the Department. With all the time and trouble involved, I really hate to see you slip away again," grimaced the civilian appointed department manager.

"Air ambulance has already been dispatched from Edmonton for these two officers. Apparently there are bigger fish than you to fry tomorrow in Edmonton," smiled the Fort Nelson department head. "So I have been instructed to offer your plane back with a gentleman's agreement that this is all kept on the QT," offered the Flight Manager.

"Hey Buds, my lips are sealed and I've forgotten this here little excursion already. You have my word on that," solemnly replied Jimmy as he extended his beaten up right hand. The promise he made to this man, for returning his beloved Jackpine Savage and lifestyle, was sealed with a firm handshake.

"Why don't you pull up to the Esso tanks over there, fuel up and get the hell out of here. Tell them to put it on our bill. We'll say the summons got lost in the accident," the head of the Fort Nelson civil aviation branch said with a grateful smile.

Preparing for a long wait, Gill had thoughtfully grabbed a quick case of Old Style when Jimmy and he left the hotel. Parking on a side road while waiting for Jimmy, Gill had been nursing the twelve pack down to a foursome. With all the action taking place on the runway, Gill figured the grounded pilot was on his way home. Sure enough within a few minutes he saw the Savage dropping out of the sky and pulling up to the flashing lights.

Pulling up in his new Ford LTD to help Jimmy refuel his spent tanks, Gill exclaimed to Midnight in amazement: "Imagine my surprise when I saw you taxi over here by your self!"

" I got to be off, Reverend," said Jimmy. "Starting to get a little too civilised around here. These guys gave me a break this time but they certainly could catch up with me again someday," reasoned the Bush Pilot. So between you and me buddy, lets just keep this incident under our hats. I had better fly the Cub into Fort St. John or Edmonton for a certificate of airworthiness, or I may end up having to ship'er by truck. I would not like to see that happen to the Savage," expounded the freed pilot. "I'll see to that as soon as my schedule slows down a bit. I got a couple of trappers that need some equipment and dogs hauled into the Fontas river."

"See you around old buddy," replied Gill. Extending his right hand, he shook Jimmy's heartily. Gill's left hand contained a bottle of car interior warmed Old Style. This he slipped into Jimmy's open, felt lined Jean jacket. "For the flight Buds," Gill smilingly said, as he bid his partner farewell.

Sitting in the big Ford, Gill watching silently as Jimmy taxied on to the strip, was thinking maybe of giving the boss a call in the morning. Those phone messages left at the front desk of the hotel by his ex-boss were no doubt about a job. "It was probably time to go back to work anyway," figured Gill. Soberly he shifted the automatic into drive and headed toward town.

Lifting off from the snow packed strip, the stealthy silhouette of the Jackpine Savage was gradually disappearing into the Northern Midnight Sky and reflecting light of the full Midnight moon.

The `Reverend Gill' reflecting back on the lonely winter's night spent in his Ford, was deciding this was a story he definitely had to relay, but would respect Jimmy's wish and for now, tell no one.

"Not only that," thought Gill,

"Who in the hell would believe such a yarn anyway!"

Thanks Gill

Epilogue

"Gill said you would know how I could contact Dawson and Sayward," I said terminating the saga. "I'd like to know what happened to that Baron and how they got it out of the bush, if they did?" I added. "I checked with D. O. T. all the way to Ottawa looking for some kind of record of this accident. To check that far back on a possible crash would be very difficult indeed, I was finally told by a lady answering the phone in both French and English; without a date and location, impossible. Nobody has been denying anything" I maintained. "There is just no record!"

"Was that one of the craft you fished out of the woods?" excitedly I asked. In my quest for more information I found a frozen silence!

"Now I know there are some stories you don't want me to print, but this is the kind of rigmarole that makes rich guys out of wannabe writers," I laughed into the phone; almost believing myself. "It's Ro-o-deee-o time partner," I exclaimed. "If Old Gill's story has an inkling of fact in it; you and I are going to be passing gas through silk." I said, censoring one of Dad's sayings describing great accumulations of wealth. "This one is the kind of yarn," I continued, "that makes legends out of old beat-up bush pilots," I concluded, finding myself running a bit at the mouth. Then getting back to the job at hand and reality of time ticking along on a collect phone call from Pink Mountain, I asked

"Dad, that high river bank, was it located on the Sikanni Chief River?"

56

Only the crackle of the northern storm travelling through a thousand miles of carrier reached my telephone receiver. Thoughts of my sixty-nine year old father, standing outside of the Mile 143 Pink Mountain Post Office, hanging frozen to the running end of a pay phone, entered my mind.

"Gill said to tell you he got his thermos back, just showed up in the mail one day," I offered, still in search of a reply. "He couldn't remember the exact year or day of the rescue but figured you could find that information in your pilot's log book."

"Oh he did, did he?" muttered the distant voice cracking along the carrier.

"Do you remember this rescue flight like that, or do you want to add anything to it?" I outright asked of my father, desperately wanting the final answer to this midnight saga of a bush pilot's lifestyle.

"Hell no!!!"   Transmitted my father's raspy voice with force and conviction! "I have logged a lot of flights in that old book over the years but I sure do not recall ever logging that one," he stated firmly.

"But it sure makes a damn good story doesn't it?"

AUTHOR'S NOTE

The Cherokee Six, sold in flight condition, was trucked by the new owner to Grand Prairie, Alberta. The bush retrieved Super Cub has been moved to it's new resting place in a farm building overlooking the Beaton River. Silently the Savage lays awaiting restoration, to again race down a bush strip and lift skyward to once more seek the freedom of the immense Northern sky.

SAVAGE ENCOUNTER

Scorching summer heat was drying out the forest, so the entire west coast logging show of Vancouver Island was shut down. Extreme fire hazard prevented man or machine from working the woods. Jim Winters and his brother Norm, owners of Ucluelet based Highline Logging, decided to drive North to Pink Mountain.

A couple of loggers hired from Port Alberni spoke much of the Pink Mountain area in which they had hunted for several years. They told the very interested Winter brothers of this bush pilot who had been flying local hunters back into the Rocky Mountains. Although hunting season would not open for some time, Jim and his brother wanted to look over the area and find a way back into the Northern B.C., sheep country. With no rain in sight, the brothers had decided to go north for a look around. If things were as the logger's stories indicated they could return another time and hopefully bag a trophy ram.

Turning left into the first driveway past the Beaton River Bridge, Jim wheeled his new truck into the naturally landscaped yard, where spotting a plane with a fellow in a cowboy hat standing beside it, decided he must have found the place. After introducing them selves, the two brothers went on to explain their venture to the cowboy pilot. The cowboy pilot indicated that he and his cousin, Melvin Peace had to move a cabin,

SAVAGE ENCOUNTER

Inger © 95

before he could take time off to fly them over sheep country. Once the cabin move was finished, the pilot would fly them over Klingzut Mountain for an eagle eye view of the Rocky Mountain terrain.

Jim offered the use of his '68 Chevrolet pick-up truck for the move and the assistance of his brother and himself in exchange for a plane ride. Over a cup of coffee the deal was made and jumping into Jim's Chev the crew of four set out to cut a few good spruce logs. These they would be placing under the building as rollers for the cabin move.

WILDLIFE

Sadie the young black bear padded down the banks of the Beaton River. Northern summer sun's rays had been absorbed by thick black fur all morning. Her attire was well suited for the cold country but Sadie was in search of a cool dip on this hot August day. Gingerly she touched the water with her snout, took a quick drink, then slipped silently into the cooling water. Wallowing in the beauty of the day Sadie had left her feeding grounds for a short time and was enjoying the luxuries of life.

Finishing her refreshing bath, she was tempting herself with a few bits of grass and then proceeded to clean the clusters of small white fruit from a dogwood patch alongside the river. Sadie was hungry and had been constantly since her birthday in late January. Pushing and tugging, Sadie and her brother had been nursing throughout the first winter. Her mother did not awaken until the call of Spring.

Shortly after the warm south winds melted the snow and softened the earth, the trio left their grass and bush-lined nest built under a large, fallen spruce tree. Having spent most of spring sleeping, the old sow would allow nursing only until the first tender grasses were sprouting life. From then on the wild siblings would be taught to fend for themselves.

Sadie's brother weighed four pounds at birth, twice that of Sadie's. When spring rolled up, the young boar cub was a seven pound bundle of black energy and would eat anything. Being larger, the male cub was always gobbling up the choicest grasses and grubs. To the timid young Sadie her big brother was a real bug-bear and becoming quite a bore. He was continually roaring around trying to catch rodents and was always better at the small amount of fishing taught to the siblings by their mother. Sadie and her brother competitively spent the summer learning to forage and a warm moist Fall had brought an abundance of berries ripe for the eating. Grubs and yellow jackets were at their prime, or one could always stop and lunch at a large ant hill full of delicate scrambling occupants. The feasting family was always storing energy and insulating fat to better survive the next long cold winter.

That second winter, Sadie and her family slept soundly until they were awakened by a warm chinook wind. Sensing spring the family of bears went for a warm winter's walk. Using a quarter of their fall weight through the long winter's sleep, when the cold spring finally came, it was almost too late for the young female bear. Pangs of stabbing hunger were quieted in Sadie's shrunken belly by the first nourishing grasses shooting up between the melting patches of snow.

Just leaving her mother's side, Sadie was fleshing out quite nicely over the summer. Still, she was a little nervous about being on her own and decided to mosey on back to the familiar open feeding area, rather than down into the river valley. Sadie liked a wide open space to graze where she could sense danger from a long distance while eating. This was important to Sadie, being on her own for the first time, she was needing the familiarity of the family feeding grounds. Unlike her brother who had left the family group almost two weeks ago, Sadie would never leave this territory in which she was born. She lumbered along a strip of abandoned Alaska Highway leading to the Sikanni Chief airstrip and her feeding grounds.

Six-thousand linear feet of U.S. Army built airstrip offering a long flat stretch of open land providing plenty of dandelions and grasses was a very productive feeding spot for the hungry bear. Frequent hunts for the elusive wild strawberries and extensive gorging on blueberries and huckleberries, went on for twenty-three hours a day through the summer. Preparing her body for the coming winter months, Sadie would continue her hyperphagic feeding until hibernation and she had no reason to wander beyond a few miles radius of the emergency landing strip. Fed by springs flowing underground from the forested Suicide Hill, the berries were plump and plentiful around the sun soaked flight strip.

With juicy berries on her mind Sadie stumbled on a rotten log on the way back from her swim. It was filled with some of the fattest grubs she had ever seen, she was stopping for a small feast. Most of Sadie's protein came in the form of ants, bees, or yellow jackets. It was hard for the young bear to catch rodents and small animals with her round, short body. Consequently, Sadie ate meat in small quantities. Being of peaceful nature she rarely used her sharp claws, big teeth and powerful muscles for anything other than ripping open a rotten stump. Her long, searching, grub-grabbing tongue did an ethnic cleansing, while blindly hunting for the smorgasbord within.

Interrupting her pre-denning feed, Sadie casually stretched her neck above the tall soap berry bush. Seeing the bright colored machine coming down the road was not frightening to Sadie. Often these huge things had gone roaring by and had done her no harm. Besides she was feeding on red berries that were suspended a little above eye level. Then curious animal things got out of the machine and were focusing their attention on her. Ignoring the commotion Sadie was continuing to feed.

Hopping out of the driver's side, Jim walked around the pick-up to where Jimmy, Melvin and brother Norm were crawling out of the passenger side of the cramped truck cab. Everybody was just horsing around and joking about the little bear. It's mother was not around, so no-one was showing too much concern.

A couple of young hunter friends of Jimmy's had stopped by early that morning on their way to Fort St. John, looking for bear hunting gear and wanted Jimmy's opinion. Jimmy jokingly stated he had enough gear right on the place to catch bear and if he should run across one, it would be tied up and waiting when the boys dropped back to the cabin later tonight. While relating the story to the group standing around the truck, a mickey of Seagrams showed up.

Watching the bear from a distance, it was Jimmy's cousin Melvin who suggested that this would be an excellent chance to grab the bear cub for when the wanna-be bear hunters returned from town. Thus showing the juvenile hunters how easy it was to get bear in the Rocky Mountains. After a few laughs, the captured adolescent bear would be released unharmed and be very little the worse for wear after the savage ordeal.

Wanting to finish the cabin move and get on with the flying Jim mentioned that the main purpose of this drive was to fall a couple of spruce about ten inches in diameter to use as rollers for moving the cabin.

"But here is an opportunity to have a little fun," replied Jimmy. "Once the cub is detained for the boys, we can whip back here and grab a couple of timber this afternoon, or later on tonight, hell, it's still light enough at midnight to fall a little spruce. Now which one of you guys is going to grab that little cub?" asked Jimmy. Courage induced by numbers, the four determined stalkers' fanned out towards the tiny she bear cub.

Poking her head out of the short brush, Sadie stood upright. To her horror, she saw the large animals were walking towards her. Sensing danger and as training dictated by her Mom, Sadie started climbing the nearest tree that would support her. Two-hundred pounds of mad mother would take care of this little matter. Once she and her brother had seen their mom tear into an old male almost twice mother's maternal size. Changing his cannibalistic mind, from having little bears for supper, to just making it out of this situation in as few pieces as possible. From this high perch Sadie, with flashing eyes, was looking forward to watching her mom perform today... Then it hit her! Mom, nor her older brother was here!

CAPTURE

At first unsure of this idea to capture the young bear, the Winter brothers were soon convinced after a couple of tugs on the small bottle of whiskey. Lots were drawn to see who was going up the tree to push or pull the bear down. Once the cub was on the ground, getting a hold on it to hog tie it would be up to the ground crew. After placing the cub in the truck box, they would haul the small critter back to Jimmy's place. There it would be kept unharmed, until the young hunters who were stopping in on their way back from Fort St John arrived. Then the young fellows would be presented with a captured bear and fulfil the commitment Jimmy had made to them earlier that day.

Odds were that someone else was going to go up and Jimmy figured this could be funny as hell. Much to the glee of his first cousin Melvin however, Jimmy lost the match and it was he who was going to have to go up after the bear. That, or face the possibility of being called 'Chicken Shit' by his peers and be known for not follow-ing up on a wager. Jimmy's thoughts raced.

"O.K. She isn't a very big bear, so what if I were to go on up and hind leg her?" thought the pilot, "when the cub turns around, a little tug and a push, with the tree leaned over from the weight? Seventy-five pounds of bear would slip from the tree to the ground. It would then be up to the ground crew to move in and subdue the wiry animal. Might be fun to watch that, perching up high, out of dangers way that is." With a smile on his face and pulling his hat firmly into place, the flying cowboy started climbing the thick limbed poplar tree.

Something strange, talking to her in a soft voice, was coming up after her. Mom had warned her about this sort of thing. Scared, the bear started climbing on up a little higher. The tree was bending with her weight. Sadie did not want to climb any higher. Below was a Savage beast more than twice her size reaching to grab her hind leg, which suddenly had developed a nervous twitch.

Bending even more Jimmy thought the tree might break off and take the bear on down to the ground crew. Then again, it might break off below both he and the bear. Jimmy did not want to end up on that hard terrain with the bear using his back as a starting block for a hasty escape. He did not want to be among the ground crew when that bear hit the turf either.

Reaching for the immature bear's hind leg, Jimmy realized the bear kept kicking, because she didn't want to go up any higher. It too had an idea the tree was about to break. Jimmy didn't want to climb up any further either, he hadn't been this high off the ground without a plane in quite some time. In a last attempt to dislodge the frightened animal, he reached out and managed to get a firm grasp on Sadie's hind leg.

Scared out of her wits, that was it for Sadie's nervous stomach and she felt her bowels loosen. The fear induced colonic produced a slimy liquid, resembling a hastily cleaned, mixed berry jam, came splashing down the tree. Containing leaves and small pieces of sticks mixed with things of protein too revolting to imagine, the gooey stuff was rapidly flowing along the branches of the poplar tree. Clinging liquid cascading across Jimmy's desperately clutching hands was gushing down his arms and little berries rolled off the end of his elbows.

Luckily most of the mess ran off the brim of his Stetson hat so his head was being protected from the onslaught. Jimmy was pleased that he had gone up well equipped for the fluid was extremely foul and he did not need that crap seeping down the back of his shirt collar. It was bad enough that while pouring down the tree the thick liquid splashed off of the branches and back up under the brim of the prized Stetson.

He didn't dare turn his head or let go of the branches he was hanging onto as he would have fallen out of the tree. Even if he had wanted to, there was no way the treed pilot was going to open his mouth to yell for help. That left him hanging about twelve feet up the slender tree, gooey and stinking to high heaven and not saying a thing. Now lightened, the juvenile bear climbed yet higher up the deciduous tree where she stayed put. Right about now, Jimmy was figuring it was about time to abandon this job.

"That little savage didn't have to dump on me like that," he thought, "I wasn't going to hurt her." Clinging tightly to the slimy, foul smelling poplar, Jimmy was belly slithering down the trunk of the tree, sounds of laughter came from below. Jimmy couldn't see what the hell was so funny, his eyes were shut tightly. Still in her lofty perch above Sadie was keeping a wary eye on all the happenings below.

Once on the ground Jimmy grabbing handfuls of grass to try to wipe the sticky goop from his face; he just knew that bear must have passed ten gallons if it passed a drop. When he could see better he noticed the only ones not laughing were he and the treed bear.

The fresh green streaks of grass mixing with the other unsightly colors, brought fresh howls of merriment from the crew now lying on the ground busting a gut.

Shortly after Jimmy noticed anytime they were talking, he'd end up having to holler over to them. No-one would stand close to him; nobody wanted to ride with him; and they were even suggesting that he travel in the back of the truck. It was kind of embarrassing riding alone in the back of the pick-up box. That is where the bear was supposed to have ridden.

When they got back to his home; he wasn't allowed in. Chucked some clean clothes from the doorway, he was told to go to the river to wash up. Fortunately it was a warm day as the river was generally chilly. Jimmy knew the heat of the day was starting to make him smell really bad but did not think he deserved this sort of treatment. Sitting in the river clad only in under wear, Jimmy began washing his body and hat with handfuls of laundry detergent. His clothes were ruined, but there was no need to throw away a perfectly good hat. Hell, he'd just gotten it shaped the way he liked it. After what that hat and he had been through, they were like old friends. Upon arrival back from the river his hat and of course the soiled clothing were immediately directed towards the burning barrel.

"That hat will not make it back into the house," declared his wife Ruby. "The way Jimmy smelled for the next little while he was damn lucky to get back in himself," she would state later. "Trying to pull a poor little bear out of a tree, imagine!"

As for Sadie she stayed up in the tree until it was safe to come down. Once on the ground, she decided she would roam with her mom and three new little sisters for a bit longer. She would soon be on her own again. Within two to five years she would have a small family of her own, starting with one or two cubs. Her mother would start another family this winter. Sadie would most likely see her mom again in the spring, unlike her brother, she would not leave her mother's home range. Like other females of her species, Sadie would claim a small part of the family range as her own.

Jim never did get that plane ride with the cowboy pilot that trip. Although he did manage to get a fly over in the morning with one of Jimmy's flying buddies, Norm and Jimmy didn't fly that day. Along with Melvin they had taken the story of the "Savage Encounter" into the wee hours of the morning. Norm got lots of pictures of his Northern bear hunting buddy.

Jimmy confessed to his comrades that the close capture had been a real learning experience. From now on he concluded, if a savage of any kind ever had him treed, he would now know exactly how to save himself.

```````````````````````````
```````````````````````````

The END.

Two years later Jim and Norm returned to the North and Jim bagged his trophy ram in the Redfern lake area twenty miles west of the Bucking Horse river lodge, Mile 175 Alaska Highway. Jim's trophy, (according to 1988 issue of Boone and Crocket) ranked the world's twentieth largest ram of the two-hundred and seventy-two that were considered large enough, to be entered in the records of The North American Big Game Book; scoring over one-hundred and eighty-two points.

ANGEL WINGS

T hree . . . Two . . . One . . . It's a lift off! Thirty-eight year old Alan Shepard was just becoming the first American astronaut to be launched into outer space: May 5, 1961. Air Force Corporal Homer Perkins would remember this day in history. Heart beating with excitement, Homer Perkins would soon be space bound himself.

Cape Canaveral Florida was way south and four time zones to the east but Homer got to hear the whole exciting launch on the local Anchorage radio station. Only a three hour time difference separated the Corporal from his home state of Missouri, he would be flying towards that Missouri destination by a Beechcraft T-34 Mentor this very morning. Admittedly Homer had some concerns about riding in a small aircraft for that distance but was saving a bundle hitching this cross country ride.

Trusting Beechcraft's T-34A to carry him east across the bottom of the 49th state, then veering south through Canada to eventually end up in the lower forty-eight, prompted a little study into the aerodynamics of the two place trainer. Close to thirty feet long the T-34 was kissin' cousin to a Bonanza. Powered with a 225 hp Continental engine it was fully equipped for aerobatics except for inverted spins. Manufacturers indicated cruise speed 173 m.p.h., top speed was 189 m.p.h.. "This little bird is quick," smiled Homer. "However Missouri is far away," conceded the young corporal to himself..

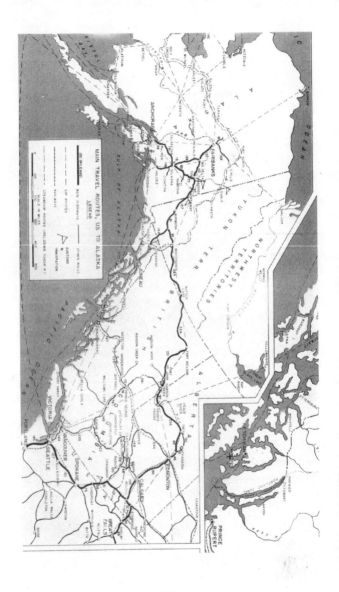

Pilot of this international flight was Flight Sergeant Bill Hickinbothem who was living on base in family quarters, Sergeant Hickinbothem had over four-hundred and fifty hours flying time acquired on several types of aircraft. What made Homer a little nervous was, less than ten of those hours were logged in a T-34. On different occasions Corporal Perkins had worked for the Sergeant, liked him and trusted his judgement. If the Sarge, a young family man, was prepared to risk the dangers of this Wilderness Flight; so was Homer.

Headlights of a car pulling up front of the Elemendorf Arrow flying Club was a signal to the Corporal that Flight Sergeant Hickinbothem had arrived. Showing up early, Homer had prepared a morning pot of coffee and sat listening to the launch while awaiting the pilots' arrival. Crushing the butt of his Lucky into an ashtray he rose to get a cup for the Sarge and noticed a tattered Milepost magazine lying on the long club coffee table. Flipping quickly through the pages he spotted a map showing their flight route from Anchorage via Seattle. "I wonder if anyone would miss this?" reflected the young corporal.

Starting quickly in the minus three degree air, the military style Beechcraft handled easily on the ground as it taxied over to the predetermined runway. Visibility, while lifting off from the headquarters of the Alaskan Air Command at 0445 hundred hours was excellent, noted the pilot levelling off the borrowed Elemendorf Flying Club craft. Navigating by compass and flying the earth's curvature, Bill Hickinbothem piloted the craft north east over Northway Junction as lights of the 13,000-acre air force base gradually faded in the distance.

Corporal Homer Perkins was anxious to get back to Missouri. Not that Homer minded his stint at the premier base in the Aerospace Defence of North America, he just wanted to get home. Stationed at the base for over a year now, Homer was aware of the base history. Since construction of the Alaskan air base in 1940, towering radar screens sat patiently watching for possible air attacks against the United States and Canada by way of Alaska. Base commander of the Alaska Air Command, also headed 'NORAD'. During an emergency, the Elmendorf base commander would immediately assume control of all military forces in Alaska.

Killed in a test plane accident in 1933 the air force base was named for Captain Hugh M. Elmendorf. It was little incidents like the captain's, that convinced Homer even more of his mother's wisdom in directing his career more towards becoming a good technician in the airforce, rather than a pilot, as his father had wanted. Father's love of aircraft ran through the blood lines and like his sire; Homer read about flight whenever he could.

Excited about his premier cross country flight, the young Corporal could see the first rays of morning light rimming the distant horizon. Behind him the westerly twinkling lights of Anchorage Alaska, dimming in the distant dark sky. Soaring across the frozen wasteland of southern Alaska the T-34 carried the crew of two through the cool clear atmosphere.

Flying in the small trainer for the first time Homer noted that the throttle, prop, and mixture controls were quadrant mounted on the left side of the fuselage. Equipped with dual stick control, the rear cockpit had a complete set of instruments to view. Within reach, Homer had everything located on the pilot's front dash, except the inverter switch that controlled the electric compass and altitude gyros. Tingling with excitement, Homer knew that with a flip of a switch by the pilot, control of the T-34 could be transferred back to him.

Although not qualified to fly an aeroplane, Homer had read everything he could about the T-34. On December 2, 1948, over a dozen years ago, the proto-type was test flown. Mentor production actually began for the US military in 1953. Between March 1950 and October 1956 the U. S. Air Force acquired three-hundred and fifty-three T-34A Mentors.

The Navy began buying the Mentors in October 1954 as a T-34B and by July 1957 had purchased 423 of the Beechcraft. Chiefly distinguishable by the yellow paint job the Navy's T-34B Mentors had the same powerhouse as the T-34A. A total of 1,904 Beechcraft T-34 Mentors were produced in a ten year period from 1948 to 1958 inclusive.

After many thousands of hours as a combination primary / basic military trainer, the aircraft were allowed to be gobbled up by the base flying clubs. Reliable as the small airship was said to be, once he was on a commercial flight home to Missouri from L.A., Homer would feel a lot better about this adventure.

Bored by the endless expanse of ice mountains and snow covered tundra with an occasional glimpse of the barren Glenn Highway, Homer started thumbing through the `Milepost' he had nipped from the flight club. Inside he studied the map showing their flight path from Fairbanks to Whitehorse. This was great, Homer could trace out his trip home. It would be good to see his little honey again, he missed mum and dad too.

Must be Northway below now, thought Homer. Instead of following the Glen we turn right and follow the Alcan highway; this is like reading a road map, decided the back seat navigator.

Using the air entry port to Alaska, as a pivot point,

77

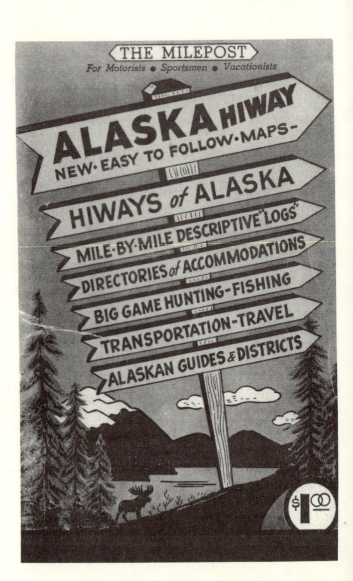

the T-34 started a gentle starboard turn to readjust it's flight path . When the bank of the plane levelled out it was flying in line with the aircraft route from Fairbanks to Whitehorse, the Canadian port of entry for flight travel.

With one eye on the compass and watching the sunrise peeking above the frozen curvature of the earth Homer could tell they were heading in a south easterly direction. Milepost map in hand and all the instruments needed right on the dash in front of his eyes, Homer figured right about now they were crossing the Alaska / Yukon border.

Flying towards the sunrise and Canadian customs, the T-34 winged across the immense landscape. Somewhat to Homer's discomfort, he could see from now on the T-34 would be travelling away from the watchful radar screens, stationed at Elmendorf.

Would any radar be tracking the plane as it travelled through the Canadian Wilderness? He asked himself. Would anyone care? Mum would! smiled Homer, recalling his mother's phone call last night, again pleading with him to give up that silly idea of travelling that far in a little wee plane.

"Your father of course doesn't agree with me," she had added. Watching the glorious colours of the sunrise light up the northern winter sky, Homer bet his dad would like to be in his place right now. Morning rays of light entering the small cab of the Mentor, prompted Homer to map out his trip home.

Lets see, we turned at Northway; destination Whitehorse, thought Homer. After landing, and a well deserved breakfast, a short flight would then take them to Watson Lake, where Bill had suggested they spend the first night of their journey. Seemed a little strange to only fly six or seven hours a day, but the pilot had cautioned him even that would be taxing after a couple of days sitting in the small cockpit. A cautious pilot, thought Homer. He liked that.

Tomorrow, a flight through British Columbia with a touch down at Fort Nelson for fuel before lunch; the second night of the journey would be spent in Fort St. John. The last leg of the Canadian crossing would take them straight into Vancouver International Airport. Clearing customs, with the international part of the trip finished, the T34 would continue on to Seattle. Deep into the United States the T-34 would complete the last lap to L.A. From there commercial airline tickets would dictate the rest of Homer's trip. "Savings on this end of the trip will be great," thought Homer gleefully.

After four and a half enjoyable flying hours from Anchorage, the pilot landed the T-34 at the Whitehorse airstrip. Sergeant Hickinbothem normally carried a 357 Magnum while travelling cross country, but had heard from flying buddies that clearing a side arm through Canadian customs was always sticky: having to put everything in a plastic bag and seal it: a lot of paperwork and stuff. Aware of the Canadians' concern for weapons, Bill did not know what might happen to his survival gun, if it was carried along. Visualising the extra hassles involved clearing customs, to the Air force Sergeant's discomfort, his aircraft was un-armed. While the T-34 was being refuelled the two grabbed a quick bite to eat at a local restaurant.

Checking the fuel invoice Bill noted fuel consumption was a tad more than he had estimated for the six-hundred and fifty mile flight from Anchorage. Between Whitehorse and Fort Nelson was only a five-hundred mile stretch, one hundred and fifty miles less than he had all ready covered, and there was still more than the forty-five minute reserve left in the tank when they landed at customs. Next fuel stop; Fort Nelson.

In the afternoon, with customs cleared and a new flight plan filed, they took off to the east towards Watson Lake. Nested just north of the Yukon / British Columbia border, Watson Lake was posted as mile 632 in the Alaska highway Milepost, noted Homer. Fatigued from the two hour flight from Whitehorse, added to the four and a half hours spent earlier in the cramped cockpit, Homer eagerly checked into a room at the bustling Watson Lake Hotel.

Early the next morning, they headed in a south easterly direction. Taxiing along the flight strip bordering Watson Lake Bill noted the similarities to a Bonanza during take off. Riding in the centre of the aeroplane and using a stick control instead of a wheel, made the military style trainer seem hotter and it felt like a racer as he left the Watson Lake strip.

Twenty minutes below the Yukon border the T-34 started hitting some heavy snow. Not to take any unnecessary chances Bill turned back to Watson Lake. Crossing the British Columbia / Yukon border was not a customs problem.

A clear blue sky on the north side of the southern storm front prompted Bill to hone his scant fifteen hours of flying skills on this military trainer. Stalls were gentle, preceded by some aerodynamic buffeting. With power on, gear and flaps up, the nose dropped at 53 knots (60 m.p.h.), while the plane continued to shake a little. Power off and clean, the stall came at 58 knots (67 m.p.h.) IAS (Indicated Air Speed). Gear and flaps down and with power off, she quit climbing at 46 knots 67 m.p.h.) and again the nose dropped from the sky, plummeting towards earth.

Although the shimmy in the aircraft was causing some concern to Homer, he got a real charge out of watching the different dials and gauges in the back cockpit seat as

81

the 'G' forces were playing havoc with his face. Enjoyable as the roller coaster ride was, his stomach became a little queasy and he began to get a little concerned with the ups and downs. Unlike the commercial flights, this craft had no lavatory facilities! Homer relaxed somewhat when the Sarge levelled out the T-34 and headed west towards the slightly visible Watson Lake.

"This would not take long now", thought Homer. Head winds that shook the small craft and resisted forward movement earlier, were now behind the aeroplane pushing it swiftly over the rugged terrain towards the Watson Lake runway.

Landing much like a Bonanza, Bill was pleased with the way the plane handled touchdown at 69 m.p.h.. Using substantially more fuel while completing stalls and other aerobatics manoeuvring that he had put the craft through, Bill checked his tank gauges; half full, two and a half hours flying time left. Lots of fuel for the less than two hour flight to Fort Nelson. Plus he still had the forty-five minutes of emergency fuel carefully calculated into the thirty-nine gallon capacity of the aeroplane's twin wing tanks.

In the early afternoon, with lunch finished, Bill decided the weather had cleared up enough to give Fort Nelson airstrip another try. From an altitude of a thousand feet he would visually follow the Alaska Highway right in to the wilderness outpost; just in case that weather came in again.

Where the Liard river broke away from the roadway, the weather worsened. Carefully scanning the commandeered Milepost magazine, Homer determined they were flying over mile 496 of the Alcan run; it was becoming more difficult to read as the small craft danced around in the head winds. At times it seemed as if the plane was just standing still as it fought for forward movement; and the Nelson strip.

Heading south in the direction of Muncho Lake the pilot dipped down towards the Alcan highway for a visual reference. Clear patches were getting smaller, the weather was pushing the aircraft closer to the roadway. It was not bad enough for the pilot to turn the T-34 back; but grim enough for the passenger to pay very close attention to what was happening.

Watching closely for a glimpse of the two lane white ribbon winding through the wilderness mountains, the air travellers flew over Muncho Lake Park. Passing over Toad River, Homer noticed the weather had lightened up a bit. "Only a hundred and eighty-four miles to Fort Nelson," thought Homer with a grim smile on his face. Hour and a half flight time; he could handle that, but was wondering if Shepard found his couch in Freedom 7 as cramping as the back of this darn little plane?

Following the Alaska highway over the summit to Fort Nelson should not have been a problem as a rule. Nor should there be a problem landing on the twisting highway any time the pilot deemed the situation necessary. Not wanting to land the sturdy craft just anywhere, Bill pushed on.

Using the highway as a visual reference more altitude was needed to follow the two lane roadway up the mountain stature to the summit pass. Swirling snow flakes plastering the wind shield of the military style cockpit became heavier, the higher up the mountain the light craft climbed, the closer it was pressed to the snow whitened highway.

With four-hundred and fifty hours under his belt Bill was trained for unusual recoveries on instruments, but was not an instrument rated pilot; nor was the craft equipped for Instrument Flight Rules. An intermittent radio was also a concern; sometimes it would receive and sometimes not. At

Watson Lake the radio was working just fine, but now? There was no sense in taking chances, Bill didn't want to fly into a clouded front. He would have to turn the craft around and hope the weather was not already closing in on him from behind!

MILE 408

Then in the darkened distance a gas station luminary shone through the northern flurries, beckoning to the lonely sky travellers. Noticing lights on each side of the highway was a deciding factor for Bill; in order to set down safely he would have to circle and watching for wires, land downhill. Just skimming under some electrical wires while descending to the gravelled highway the T-34 tires touched land. Quickly the craft was brought to a stop just before the narrow meandering winter roadway started curving off to the left into the timber. On the Alaska highway that evening Bill made a real tight emergency landing, just as the mountain range socked in for the night.

Homer happily jumping out and lifting the tail section was physically turning the aeroplane around. It was now facing in the direction in which it had come in for the landing. Electing to walk the short distance to the gas station, Homer was following in the swirling snow kicked up by the T-34 while taxiing down the rough roadway. Bill was parking the craft alongside the small stopping place by the time Homer was walking up the snow covered driveway.

After a rough one hour flight from Watson Lake then a squeaky tight landing, the two men were now in a borrowed car driving down the dark, snowy, mountain highway to Milepost 397. Using the telephone at Rocky Mountain Auto Court Bill phoned the D.O.T. informing them that he was not following the original flight plan but would call again in the morning with an update on his plans depending on weather.

"Depending on the weather!" fumed a disillusioned Homer. Staring past the headlights of the old automobile into the reflection of the swirling flakes, he could barely see the faint tire imprints left on the lonely snow covered roadway. Down in the mouth, the young man on a three week leave was realizing the one-car gas station could be home for quite sometime.

"This place is so small it didn't even make the Milepost," steamed Homer. Settled in at the small truck stop for the night, things got better when Bill and Homer met air force folks from Elmendorf, who were stopping for dinner.

"Yes, Alan Bartlett Shepard Jr. was fine as well as was the condition of Freedom 7" replied the Alaskan gentleman to Homer's questions. "Shepard made his historic flight less than a month after Major Yuri Gagarin of the Soviet Union had orbited the earth in the world's first manned space flight," the informed man was explaining. "Shepard never circled the earth like Major Gagarin did. Rocketing 117 miles straight up from Cape Canaveral it only took fifteen minutes air time before he landed three-hundred and two miles out in the Atlantic ocean!" The self-professing amateur rocket scientist was proclaiming to the very attentive Homer.

"Unlike Major Gagarin's space craft," carried on the American gentleman, "Alan had manual control of his one ton space capsule during the re-entry flight. Laying on a contoured couch, Shepard had been pressing Freedom 7 to a top speed of 5,180 miles per hour while re-entering the earth's atmosphere, enduring forces twelve times that of earth's gravity at surface."

After dinner and a pleasant conversation, Bill asked the south bound Elmendorf couple if, when they reached Fort Nelson, they would phone the Department of Transport and inform them that the T-34 was coming in to the airport before noon tomorrow. Then if for some unforeseen reason the Beechcraft did not arrive on time, the Fort Nelson Department would automatically be alerted to possible craft difficulties. If the weather did get bad, Bill would drive back down the eleven miles of twisting gravelled highway to Rocky Mountain House Lodge before noon and phone to suspend his flight plan again.

Confident the plane would be refuelled and well on it's way towards Fort St. John by lunch time, Bill indicated to his American Air Force friend that reaffirming his flight plan was very likely a useless gesture. However, it was better to be on the safe side. What the heck, Bill was a responsible pilot!

"Not having to make a phone call to D.O.T. in the morning made sense," thought Homer, as he ground his third to last Lucky Strike into the ashtray sitting next to his coffee cup. "That would save another bumpy car trip to Rocky Mountain Lodge," he reasoned. By the pilot's actions, Homer could tell that the Flight Sergeant was reluctant to tax the generosity of the owners of the gas station once more, by borrowing their only means of transportation. Besides in the time they would spend travelling that twisted gravelled road by car to make an unnecessary phone call, they could already be landing the T-34 at Fort Nelson.

"This is going to be a great trip," decided Homer, pulling fresh smelling sheets up to his chin. "Watson Lake Hotel this is not," jokingly Homer said to Bill who lay on the opposite bed. Adornment of the accommodation consisted of two single width beds sharing furniture space with a home-made night table. Fresh air flowed from a small window, neatly trimmed with frilly curtains. Located in the back of the isolated gas station, the small quarters were providing the men a warm place to spend the night. Deep pulsating rhythm, from the heat dispensing diesel motor driving the electrical generator, lulled the weary men into a deep sleep.

TAKE OFF

Directing the aircraft as far down the road as possible while watching for traffic, Homer was looking apprehensively at the power lines crossing the T-34's emergency flight strip. Helping Bill turn the plane around manually, he could see they would be needing maximum distance for takeoff. Then climbing up into the cockpit and huddling in the back seat of the cold vibrating plane, it was looking to Homer like another cramped flying day was about to begin, "If we make it over those wires that is?" worried Homer. "Saving a few buck's on a commercial flight maybe had not been such a good idea after all."

With rays from the rising sun filtering through the wind shield warming the cockpit greenhouse, the T-34 was ready for takeoff. Thirty-three feet of Beechcraft wing span didn't leave a lot of clearance on either side of the narrow roadway and the mountain altitude had to be close to four thousand feet. Sweating it out a little, Bill could not help but notice those power lines hanging above the road.

Shoving the throttle full forward, the 225 Continental hungrily sucking in the thin mountain air mixing with full rich fuel, instantly spun the full low pitch prop to twenty-six-hundred rpm. Clawing through the high mountain air for land speed, the labouring propeller was quickly pulling the metal aircraft down the improvised gravel strip. Rising steadily the airspeed indicator seem to have difficulty reaching the sixty Knot mark the T-34 was needing to become airborne. Engine revving wide open the craft was almost reaching sixty-nine miles per hour while speeding along the Alaska highway. Strung tautly some twenty feet in the air the back electrical wires were silhouetted against the white mountain background;

"If you don't come off now," demanded Bill of the land craft, "we won't make it over them wires!" It was now or never! Easing the Joy stick back tightly to his uneasy stomach, and the nose wheel of the T-34 was airborne. At a rate of climb to thirteen-hundred feet per minute, the small craft was scrambling for altitude and freedom of the sky. The back landing gear barely skimming over the black wires.

Heart beating wildly, Bill set the rpm with the prop control to 2,400 rpm, producing a climb rate of 900 feet per minute, these settings adjusted air speed of the ascending Beechcraft to 100 knots (115 m.p.h.). Minutes after nine o'clock while trimming the T-34 off for a smooth cruise at 6,500 feet Bill set the flight course on a compass heading East, towards Fort Nelson. Estimated Time of Arrival ten-hundred hours.

Sufficient fuel was left in the wing tanks for the one hour flight to Fort Nelson. Forty-five minute reserve, added to one and a half hours flight fuel, would equal two hours and fifteen minutes flying time. "That is a good safety margin," smiled the pilot to himself, "twice what we need." More aviation gas would be obtained at the Fort Nelson strip. Propelling across the rugged wilderness at 150 m.p.h., after refuelling in Fort Nelson, the T-34 would be landing at the Fort St. John airport by early afternoon.

Near Summit Lake the weather was down again; scattered and broken. Before Bill was aware of it, the T-34 was above an overcast. Pressing forward and taking the modified Bonanza Beechcraft to 11,500 feet he was follow-ing the low frequency radio range emitting from the Fort Nelson repeater station. Listening to the air traffic conversa-tion over the radio waves, D.O.T. talking to pilots far below the Beechcraft. Bill calling out in intermittent intervals, was never to receive an answer.

As impressive as the raw beauty of the clouds forming around the mountain tops was; Homer was beginning to become concerned about coming down. Thick cloud looked like miles of snow laying across the land, Homer felt almost as if he could jump into the white mass and land in powder. Reality was Homer knew that he would not be held by the fluffy air mass but allowed to tumble on through until somewhere there would be the side of a mountain. Homer sure hoped the Sarge knew where they were cause he had not seen land for almost an hour now and this Milepost map wouldn't work unless they could see the highway.

Summit Lake was an elevation of 4230 feet and being the highest section of the Alaska highway Bill was figuring the ceiling and the top of summit pass were very close. If he could not find land soon, he would have to chance a spin through the giant cumulus. He should be able to make it through all right. If he came out on a high mountain like the Summit, it could get tricky; dropping down on top of a Cessna full of people out for a joy ride, was also a hidden risk Bill did not care for.

Realizing that constantly seeking favourable weather conditions at different elevations, was expending most of the precious craft propellant, Bill found himself checking the fuel gauges again. The Beechcraft was coming down at some point; he was praying that it would be on the Fort Nelson strip.

Then, an opening in the clouds revealed a river valley thousands of feet below. Deciding his bearings were right Bill elected to buff the overcast, hoping the valley did not have high cloud hidden mountain banks. If he didn't take this window there might not be another.

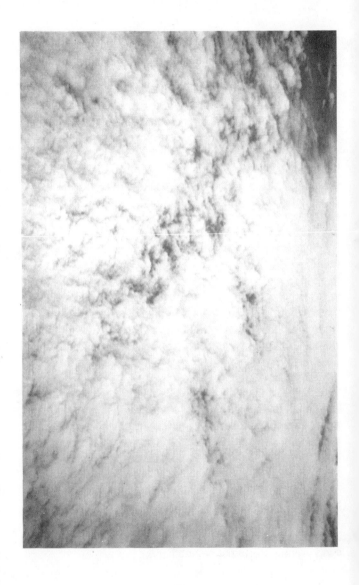

With less than thirty minutes flying time before he would be using the forty-five minute reserve, Bill began spiralling the T-34 towards the rapidly closing gap in the thick cloud formation. Screaming in protest at one-hundred and fifty knots per hour, the governors kicking in were holding the two-hundred and twenty-five horse motor from over revving. Through seven thousand feet of swirling air mass the aircraft was descending into the foggy shifting view of the frozen terrain, in a frenzied plunging towards earth. Bill convincingly told himself he could fly through the cloud this way. The likelihood of hitting somebody in the air away out here had to be very low; the side of a mountain on the other hand was readily available.

"How much cloud formation had Alan Shepard ripped through, when the Redstone rocket launched Freedom 7 into deep space?" wondered Homer as he sat staring into cloud formation just outside of his cockpit window. "Did Shepard have this feeling of impending doom in his gut when freedom 7 was detached and like Homer's craft hurled towards earth?"

Levelling out safely under the overcast, the relieved pilot was not exactly sure where they were. Straight ahead Steamboat Mountain was looming behind the wispy shifting low Stratus cloud formation. Then Bill saw the river.

"Muskwa," the name leapt to his tongue. "I remember the river on the flight chart," thought Bill. Turn left at Steamboat, that was the game plan when he first mapped out the flight. The Alaska Highway would run along port side as he followed the Muskwa River right on in to Fort Nelson. Highway obscured by fog, Bill was electing to follow the river valley and hoping the cloud would be staying high enough above the river valley for him to reach the airstrip. Thankfully it looked like they would be landing before having to use any of the forty-five minute reserve. Bill didn't care to push his luck in this isolated North country.

Surviving a heart stopping dive through the clouds renewed Homer's confidence levels and appetite. He had thoughts of coffee and possibly a roast beef sandwich at Fort Nelson, then after refuelling, a short two hour flight into Fort St. John. "Heck, maybe the pilot would shoot for Prince George if the weather was good this afternoon," thought Homer.

Unable to identify any land marks on the chart, the pilot was starting to doubt his decision to follow the river. By Bill's reckoning they should have been in Fort Nelson, at the least, twenty minutes ago. If his fuel calculations were accurate, he was ten minutes into his forty-five minute reserve!

Rolling hills below were marred by a large burn that had gone through a few years before. On the chart where Bill decided they were, six tractor trails were shown. In reality the landscape looked like a rat's maze in a laboratory! Many more fire trails had been cut since the mapping of the chart. Although all the trails seemed to travel in straight lines of Latitude and Longitude, Bill saw in despair there was no way to figure the maze or flight map out.

After an hour of staring out the side window looking for an airport, Homer was starting to tire of the view. Alan only had a fifteen minute trip up for a look at the world's landscape. Homer was wondering if the view from Freedom 7 was as desolate as his. When the US Astronaut came back to earth, it was over nice soft water. All Homer had seen speeding beneath the aircraft at over a hundred nautical miles per hour were trees and rock and more trees and rock. Surely radio contact from Cape Canaveral would be clear, not faint like Fort Nelson! Receiving garbled conversations, the pilot always calling, transmissions received? Not by Fort Nelson! Who then? Who could hear them? Who would answer? Calling more calling. Somebody answer. Possibly they were not far from the most northern town in B.C. and its haven runway. But which way? How far??

Glancing at the fuel gauges, Bill could see both registering near the empty mark. They had to be in the vicinity of Fort Nelson. Fog, obscuring focal points for some time now was making it almost impossible to estimate where the craft was positioned on the map?

Location for now, unknown. Travelling at one hundred and thirty knots with retractable landing gear in place, it would not take long before he could be sure of his position. Then again, fuel supply was dictating he didn't have long.

Ahead, about five miles, there was a tractor trail. Unlike the other miles of surveyed fire cut-lines that Bill had seen today, this straight piece of fire access roadway had a level stretch. It was the only level spot without a covering of spruce tree, rock or muskeg, that Bill had seen for awhile. Then he noticed the Muskwa River diminishing to a stream. Now how did that happen? That's when it hit him! Confused for a moment when he left the cloud at Steamboat, he had turned the wrong way on the river. He had been flying upstream for forty minutes, instead of down river towards Nelson.

Quickly finding his location on the flight map he figured the Beechcraft had to be within eighty miles of Fort Nelson if he cut across country through the fog. Gauges showed the aircraft did not have that much fuel left. The manual said there should still be twenty minutes of flying time left when the tanks read empty. Shifting wind speed and direction seemed to vary the float gauges, so Bill

couldn't be certain how much gas was left in the wing tanks.

Trutch! It was forty miles to the west. With less than twenty minutes fuel supply left at one-hundred and fifty miles per hour it would be close. They could eventually cross the Alcan highway, at this point Bill would gladly try any kind of landing on a gravelled strip. The aircraft might be over trees instead of the highway when the T-34 eventually ran out of fuel. Certain death? Bill did not want to speculate. There could be a better than even chance of dying with a branch through your head. Not necessarily, but maybe. In amongst the small spruce scattered about the level cut line straight a head, Bill figured he could land safely.

TOUCHDOWN

"I'm going to ask you now," Bill said to Homer. "We can do a touch down here where I can land it, or we could take a chance and go for it. I think we are very close to the Alcan, but if I am wrong, we might have to set down in a very unfavourable place. I want you to have your say in this," explained Bill.

What was the pilot saying? Run out of gas! Homer had run out of fuel in the farm truck before, it had been a real inconvenience. Several miles he had walked to the farm and returned carrying a five gallon can full of gas; ruined his whole day. What happens when you run out of fuel in an aeroplane? Land safely now or close to a strip later?

Close to a strip later? What the heck did close to the strip mean? Hand grenade training films had shown Homer that close worked with them. Many games tossed with his dad on their Missouri farm had shown the youth that close counted also in Horseshoes. But there was no way he could see how CLOSE to a strip would work with the landing of an aircraft.

Interest in ever setting down on any strip not paved had diminished with the highway landing last night. Definitely he did not want to land out in the middle of nowhere on a small chunk of land scattered with Christmas trees but then again he did not want to crash close to a strip either. Seemed like no matter which choice he made it would involve a real change in his style of life. Decisions, Homer decided, he did not need at this moment and said. "You decide!"

Responsible not only for this craft owned by the Elmendorf Air Force Base Aero Club, W. Hickinbothem pilot-in-command of Beechcraft T34 aircraft, registration N1403Z, was also responsible for the well being of his passenger and this plane was coming down soon, that was for sure.

"Okay," committed the pilot. "I'm going in."

Assuming the crash position he had practised the day before at the service station, Air Force Corporal Homer Perkins hoped it would not be his final stance as he felt the plane gliding gently towards earth. Freedom 7, endured forces twelve times stronger than the force of gravity. Homer surmised Alan Shepard must have felt a similar sensation running through his guts, when his craft plummeted to earth.

Shepard had many radar eyes watching for his space ship, Homer didn't know who, if anyone, would be watching for the air ship they were in. Suspended at Rocky Mountain Auto Court by phone, re-filing of the flight plan was now in the hands of the young family couple driving to Fort Nelson this morning.

Homer wishing now they had made that trip one last time down the eleven miles of gravelled road and made that phone call themselves to the Fort Nelson Department Of Transport. Homer was down in the mouth; this was holidays. He was just on leave going down to the states to see his girl.

Flying to Los Angeles in the Beechcraft had been a good money saving idea. From Los Angeles, a short commercial flight home to Missouri and his Mary-Lou. It had been a great plan but Homer promised himself if he ever flew again, it would be in a much bigger plane. That is if he ever had the opportunity to fly again.

"If you are going to land on an unprepared strip," Bill remembered from reading the Beechcraft manual, "raise the gear and belly land." Sitting on seat chutes that were real hard," Bill reasoned, "if the T-34 didn't make a smooth landing, the sudden impact could break the back of either man." A broken back out here would result in absolutely no chance of survival. Using the landing gear as a cushion would soften the blow when touching earth. Bill decided if it wiped off, well it wiped off. At this time he was concerned about life rather than the craft.

Gliding the metal Mentor through the air the pilot brought the aircraft in as slowly as possible over the bush strip. Keeping the power on and landing flaps in place, he flew nose up at stall speed of sixty m.p.h. touching the wheels of the Beechcraft down onto the bulldozed path. The frozen two inch diameter trunks, of the small trees snapped, as the winged invader cleared the naturally reforested strip.

It was a warm 7th of May day and beneath a soft crust of ice, the snow was melting as the one and one-half ton of craft came down in the wilderness. Retracting from the wings the landing gear dug in a bit and then the nose gear came down, digging into the snow. Soon a large mass built up in front of the craft and the nose landing gear snapped off bringing the T-34 skidding to a halt, in less than a hundred feet. Opening the canopy and yelling, "get out!" Bill was climbing out on the wing the same time Homer was happily jumping towards earth.

It was a fine landing, Homer really didn't know what was going on or what had happened to the plane, but he thought it was a great landing! He would have been pleased with anything, he was alive. Right now, that's all he cared about. Heart racing, Homer was finding things pretty interesting again.

After making sure there was no possibility of fire, the downed pilot climbed back onto the nine and one-half foot high craft and grabbing a parachute seat tossed it to the ground. Popping it open, the chute was hung from the rudder exposing the international orange side, so it could be seen from the air, the white day glow underside lay against the snow. Placing rocks in the parachute back pack and on the chute edges, prevented the silk fabric from bunching up in the slight breeze.

Removing fairings from the motor encasement, Bill started placing them in the snow forming a three point triangle. Pouring a quart of oil evenly into each of the cowling, provided a container for the aviation fuel drained from the T-34 fuel line. The quart can full of fuel stood at ready. Should the opportunity arise to light a signal fire, gas would be added to the standing oil. Igniting the mixture with the strike of a match, a signal fire could be had in an instant. Allowing plumes of oil blackened smoke to snake upwards, sending the international three point distress signal for help into the clear northern atmosphere, .

Rescue beacon set up and back in the solar warmed cockpit, Bill could still hear the D.O.T. radio transmissions clearly. Although he tried calling over and over, he could not raise the Fort Nelson Airport. They simply were not receiving him.

Climbing out of the plane's greenhouse and gazing into the magnificent beauty of the raw wilderness and white capped mountains in the distance; perhaps not wanting to break the still silence, he said in awe under his breath. "Oh Lord, if this is the last place in the world you have chosen for me to see, you sure picked a beautiful spot."

Studying philosophy at this time in his life, up until today everything in the young aviator's religion had just been a matter of discussion and deliberation. But this; this was the real challenge.

"This is it, a test of your faith," Bill said to himself. "You either believe or you do not." The young pilot surprisingly seemed to be at peace inside. Brought to a standstill in his busy life, he asked with private prayer, "why am I here?" Then for the first time in Bill's life the Lord spoke to his heart.

"I will let you know." Again a short time later Bill heard himself trying to appeal to his Saviour.

"Well look," he said. "Lord, you know I'm young," stated Bill. "If I make it out of here I'll be thirty in July and I have a family," he added. "There's a lot more that I can do " rationalized Bill. "I will quit smoking and I will quit drinking liquor," bargained Bill. "There is so much more, for me to do! He affirmed. Please; just get me out of here!!" Quietly to Bill's racing heart came a reply.

"Don't give me that! If you were sixty-five and standing there, you would be saying the same thing," came the silent message.

An hour or so after the forced landing, the two men started an exploratory walk up the tractor trail they had landed on. It seemed to end a ways up and they wanted to see if there was a cache or anything like that left behind by the bulldozer crew. Walking about three miles and finding nothing but a wall of trees where the trail ended, they headed back to the busted plane.

On the flight chart, there was a little black square identified as an Indian Village, it was about five miles or so from where the two men thought they were. It seemed ridiculous for them to just stay there by the aeroplane and not at least check it out. At the Indian community they could find shelter and food. "But which trail? Was help only five miles away?" questioned Bill of himself. "Would the village still be there?" The answer would have to wait until morning.

According to the aircraft's outside air temperature gauge the northern spring air was dropping to minus four degrees Fahrenheit. With no interior heat other than the minimal body warmth of two cold men, the southern raised Missouri born lad knew sleeping in this wilderness bunk house would be the coldest nights sleep he had as of yet, ever endured. Transmitting through the metal fuselage, the dark cold seemed to penetrate Homer's warmest body parts.

The chill was warded off last evening by a nice warm little room, tonight rhythmic pounding of the generator's diesel would not be heard. The silence would be broken only occasionally by the lonesome howl of a timber wolf. Nor would there be a big breakfast waiting come daylight. Just a walk in the woods, somewhere?

"Don't be wandering around in those northern woods," Homer could remember his mum saying, "you'll become a bear's dinner!" His mum began warning him about Polar bears and Kodiaks as soon as she heard where he was stationed. Homer found himself wondering how mum would feel if she knew that right now, he was surrounded by packs of man killing Wolves, with no means of defending them selves.

By putting his feet up on the instrument panel, Homer found a surprisingly comfortable position. Cramping as the cockpit was, metal fuselage made a lot of sense. Bears couldn't rip through metal. Could they?? A walk to find the Indian village in the morning, then what? He couldn't bring himself to contemplate where he might be sleeping tomorrow night. He was secretly hoping it would not be in the bush!

Unless the suspended flight plan had been re-filed, Bill realized that the chance of D.O.T. looking for them soon was slight. Someone flying over by chance in this remote wilderness, unlikely. If his pinpointing of this location was done accurately, they were way south of the flight path from Watson Lake to Fort Nelson.

A stray flight might pass over while involved with the search, but Bill knew that was unlikely. After search and rescue were through exploring the large areas around the flight route, they would be abandoning the search. The official accident report would be assuming that the plane had been lost somewhere beneath the forest canopy. Or that it had simply disappeared into one of the small lakes nesting in the many square miles of untamed wilderness separating the two isolated northern towns.

Being forty or fifty miles east of the flight route from Fort Nelson to Fort St. John, a chance sighting of the crash site by a commercial aircraft: slim. Nor would D. O. T. be searching this area below Fort Nelson for a long time; if ever.

"Homer did not have to know," thought Bill. "He was a good kid and did not need any bad news tonight." Working as technician for the Alaskan radio forces network Homer had worked for him on different projects. He was a level headed kid but didn't seem too positive in this predicament of doom and gloom.

Working part-time in commercial television, Bill was known by a number of people in Anchorage. Moonlighting as a news and weather man, he was supplementing military forces income to support his growing family. Operations director of the U.S. forces network, Bill Hickinbothem was sort of obligated to use a fictitious name over civilian air waves. Smiling, he thought of the many times fellows working with him on the base, would comment on how much he resembled Bill Kelly the weather guy on television.

Gazing up through the canopy into a clear night Bill marvelled at the many lights in the wide sky. It was as if a darkened mirror was reflecting a city's luminaries down onto this remote stretch of wilderness. The light casting a frozen sheen over the snow covered landscape.

"How are the media going to handle this incident?" Bill was wondering. Jumping out of the newspaper in bold black print, the paper's head lines to Bill's mental vision read:

'LOCAL PILOT LOST IN WILDERNESS.' Days later the report read;

'Search Continues,' on Page three. By the end of the week a small caption next to the comic section stated search and rescue were;

'Calling search off,' because of abnormal weather. On the back page two weeks after Bill's mishap, subscribers still interested would read:

'Search Abandoned.'

Thinking of his wife, his thoughts went to the intersection on two busy Anchorage streets outside the bank where she was employed. In his mind's eye, Bill could see the traffic pulling up to the red light and stopping. At the green signal, the city traffic continued on.

"If I die here, my death won't even slow traffic," thought Bill. "What purpose has my life served?" He loved his family and had left financially what he could, so he didn't have any guilt about that. But leaving his young family alone was tugging at his heart. Should he have spent more time with them? He tried so hard to get them what they were needing. If only he could see his six year old boy! Or hold his young daughter, for just a moment. Slowly his eyes started to close. Wait! He could not doze off. What if a plane flew over? Signal fires at night would be spotted for miles. Besides it was too cold to sleep anyway.

NEXT MORNING

Early morning heat radiating throughout the cock pit warmed the freezing men as they tried to read the map indicating a village to be close by, a walkabout to find the Indian reserve was soon in the planning. The land was deceptive however and when finishing the climb to the top of the first rise, all the men could see in front of them was the next rise; with a small valley lying in between. On they walked.

The spring snow was crusty and on the ground in large amounts. Where it was shady all day, the two men could scoot along the top of the frozen terrain. In spots of few or small trees, the solar heat warming the sun sensitive snow was causing it to become soft in some places. After a few steps, suddenly one foot would break through the thick crust and plunge knee deep in snow. By early afternoon the muskeg started to soften wherever land lay open to the continuous spring sun. Feet wet, the two men became sticky hot soon after the constant exposure to the Northern brightness. Entering the shady patches of forest they were immediately chilly again. It was tough going.

In the sun, one dare not open ones mouth or breath through the nose without protection. Mesmerizing clouds of mosquitoes were following them, Bill had never seen anything like it in his life. It was scary. If you fell down and quit, there would be nothing left of you but your dog tags. "I've just got to get out of here," thought Bill. "Where do these

things live? It's all snow. There's so much snow, do these guys live under it or what? Where do they all come from?" he screamed mentally; trying vainly to drown out the constant buzzing of thousands of mosquitoes swarming to find a piece of flesh and drill for blood.

"These little creatures could actually eat you alive," thought Homer, frantically wiping the small bodies from his sweaty neck while trudging along behind the pilot. People went crazy in the bush he had been told, No-See-Ums flying up the nose was irritating but the constant buzzing in the ears was enough to drive you nuts, just before having all the blood sucked out of your body. Incredible!

Wet socks slipping down soaking leather boots continually exposing snow chilled ankles, was kind of messing up Bill and Homer's feet. Half the time the woollen socks ended up as a sodden clump around the men's snow numbed heels. Sitting around the smoky fire, drying socks and stuff, Bill was thinking how nice it would be to have a bite to eat for lunch.

It was obvious this kid from Missouri had not been in the north very long and just didn't have any wilderness experience. "A real good guy," thought Bill. Although not complaining, Homer was probably very hungry and did not seem to be enjoying this little hike much and Bill was just wishing he had a bit to eat for his young friend, that would perk him up. Suddenly, some barking.

"Listen," quieted Homer, "there's a moose barking." Bill thought for a minute and said.

"Homer, moose don't bark." Homer thought a minute, then said.

"Bears bark."

"Yup, they sure do!" exclaimed Bill.

Homer was bear aware. Mum had made sure of that

and good sized tracks in the snow had been pointed out by Bill. The Grizzly print edges had been burned back by the melting sun, making the mammoth indentations even larger. Some of the bear tracks Homer had seen today were big enough to hold a forty footer upright. He did not want to end up bear pucky on some animal trail. He hoped he would see his mo-mmo-omom again!

Not having a weapon he noticed Bill had already cut a sapling and sharpened one end. Seeing the other man armed, Homer decided a stick of his own might be handy for walking. For fighting a Grizzly set on lunch, he would have preferred something a bit more substantial in the way of a weapon. God he missed Missouri and his folks.

"We ought to go back," said Bill. "The chart indicates we are close to the village, but the manual says we have to stay with the aeroplane."

"Whatever you want to do," replied Homer. Uncomfortable as the plane was, sleeping in the wilds with out the protection of the twenty-nine and a half foot metal barracks was something Homer really did not want to do.

"Okay, we are going back," said Bill. Turning around quickly, so that Homer would not see the disappointment etched in his face, Bill started walking towards the downed aircraft. Finding the village would have meant a new try at life but if the men were to survive for any length of time, they would have to conserve their energy.

Bill had now come to understand a whole new sense of values while stranded in the northern wilderness, time lines and activities that directed his lifestyle before the set down had stopped. With nothing else to do he had time for thinking and reflecting. Nothing could distract him out here: no radio's, no schedules, no yard to look after, no car to maintain. He did not have to set aside time for meals.

Personal hygiene was not even time consuming, leaving Bill with lots of spare time on his hands for philosophy!

Last night he realized that food should not be taken for granted: their hunger had not been satisfied by the shared Babe Ruth bar and package of Planters nuts Bill had found in a search of his flight bag. Then thinking about his comfortable home in Elmendorf, Bill understood that a house was not just a place to invite your friends: It was protection from miscellaneous animals and a world that is not all that pleasant sometimes. Folks don't think about that, enough. Proper clothing was very important for survival too. Thankfully both he and Homer were well outfitted for dress in issued flight clothing right down to the leather military boots.

Trudging steps behind the pilot, Homer could see Bill was no longer sure of himself. By this time he was entirely dependent on the man who had got him out of that cursed sky. Homer made a mental note to never fly again. Now could Bill save him from this ground predicament they were in. Looking on the bright side, Homer affirmed at least he was still alive. For how long he did not want to guess.

Homer thought he heard Bill murmuring something back at him but could not be sure. It was impossible to hear over his heavy breathing and the constant crunching of the crystallized snow Homer was always ploughing through. He would just follow behind. Suddenly, the leader stumbled to his knees and to Homer's horror, did not get up.

Leading the way back to the plane, the magnitude of their predicament overwhelmed Bill. They were lost, very likely well off of the travelled air routes. The Lord's Prayer played on Bill's lips, cold reality stabbed at his inner being, he now fully understood the hopeless predicament they could very well be in. Bill had reached "Thy will be done" in his personal prayer, then stumbling to his knees in fatigue

"Angel Wings"
Uniju 95.

and humbly lifting his face skyward, with a quiet plea through lips parched by the dry cold air, Bill petitioned the Heavens.

"Lord, I'm not trying to make any deals with you, cause I do not think you want to bargain. Not that I have much to bargain with anyway, but I do want to tell you this . . . If you should see your way clear to get us out of here alive, I will try to do something more meaningful with my life. Much more than I have done up until now."

As the prayer drifted through the northern silence Homer saw the irony of the situation, not only was God leaving this Missouri farm boy to die in the Great Canadian North, he had to go out with some religious nut.

Then he heard an aeroplane. This was starting to get so corny the young Missouri man couldn't believe it, the wilderness was beginning to play with his mind! "Ha, ha," was he was going to go crazy before he died along side the ex-pilot, "ha,a,..?" But wait... The noise was growing still louder! There was no doubt about it. Homer hollered at the top of his air dried voice. "It's an Aeroplane!"

Homer started running toward Bill screaming. "I don't care what you say, you crazy S. O. B., I see an aeroplane. You brought us an aeroplane!" Jerking a towel covering his head to protect his face from the hordes of mosquitoes Homer was waving it like a flag towards the departing aircraft flying overhead. Sending his flight cap flying into the soggy snow covered muskeg.

CF-JST decals leapt into view from the under wing of the aircraft roaring up over the small rise. Levelling out at less than fifty feet above the heads of the bewildered men, the Jackpine Savage indicated the men had been seen by wagging it's wings. "The sight couldn't have been more beautiful had it been flying with the wings of an angel," Bill would later say. "It was a wonderful miracle."

Contracted by Don Peck, the Savage was to fly into the Tuchodi Lake area, drop off gear and several cases of canned food then bring a camp attendant, who was left behind to square up the camp buildings, back to Trutch. Getting things ready for Peck's next hunting season the attendant had elected to forego the three day pack trip by horse in favour of the forty minute plane ride. Usually the flight path would not have been over this remote area, the short flight to Trutch Mountain along the familiar Alaska Highway being preferred. At Trutch the Savage would have then headed off into the wilderness towards Peck's hunting territory. Pressing family matters at Pink Mountain Lodge had put the flight time of the Savage a little behind schedule and scarce spring daylight hours dictated the shorter route towards the Rocky mountain divide.

Off to the pilot's left a glitter caught his attention. Rays of sunshine were reflecting from the crystallized snow that had become 'mirror like' from the day's thawing. Night freezing would soon transform the sheen into an eerie moonlit glossiness. Come daybreak, the crystals would again be reflecting in all directions once more. Countless times, while flying the north country, the pilot had seen this phenomenon and carried on.

Another flash and then that nagging feeling! If he wasn't in such a damn hurry he would go over and have a look. That flash again, it was almost like a signal beckoning; come back. That flash was too bright for snow or ice reflection. There it was again, about ten miles to the west.

With the instinct of a raven honing in on a shiny object, the Jackpine Savage jockeyed a ninety degree turn to port. Watchful eyes of the remote North wavered not. Tight flight plan altered for the moment, Jimmy 'Midnight' Anderson went to have a little look around.

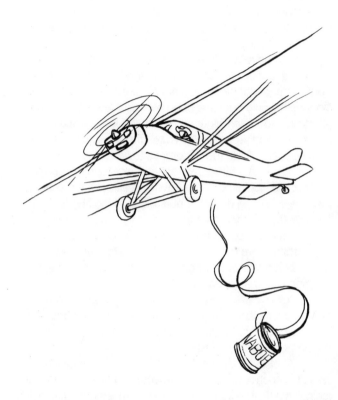

"Hot Coffee
Inga 9."

"What the hell, that kid Peck left to close the place down had already been in there ten days longer than expected. If he hadn't started walking out by now, a few more minutes won't hurt him any," rationalized the Bush Pilot.

Against the white background of snow the brightly coloured parachute draping over the wing was gently fluttering in the breeze, marking the downed aircraft's position. Circling and gliding in low while checking for occupants Jimmy, observing the brown colouring of the aircraft noted that it was a damn good thing the chute had been hung. The craft did not look damaged other than sitting on the ground nose down but no one was inside the cockpit. Identification markings read N1403Z.

"Not from this neck of the woods," thought Jimmy. "From the looks of the landing tracks that plane let down in the last little while." May 3rd a light snow fall was followed by intermittent rain. Then the temperature dropped to fifteen degrees below zero, immediately transforming the landscape into a frozen white glaze. "This set down has happened since the 3rd," reasoned Jimmy. "These skid marks look fresh."

Before setting out in search of the Indian village, to show in which direction they were walking, Bill laid some saplings out in the snow in an arrow pattern, in case some aircraft did fly by. Sun reflecting from the metal craft, had been melting the snow from around the plane. Like sticks tossed by a child, the carefully constructed rescue directions lay on the melting muskeg.

No bodies at the crash site indicated one or two people were walking out. Automatically the Savage was set into a circular search pattern. There in the snow! Tracks made by two men walking separately. Good, no one seriously injured by the rough set down. Once the direction of travel had been determined, it was only moments before the figures of one man kneeling in the snow and the other frantically waving his arms, passed beneath the belly of the Jackpine Savage. Circling, Jimmy came back around and tilting the Savage dropped a small package with a length of fluttering ribbon attached to it out the side window towards the two men.

Watching closely as the trailing red tail ribbon of the plummeting capsule was fluttering rapidly in the gravity created wind stream, Homer was wondering, "did the retrievers of Freedom 7 find it as exciting when their capsule was fluttering down from space? I doubt it," thought Homer, a big boyish grin forming on his fatigued and haggard face.

"I'm going to live!" Eight feet from the isolated men the welcome airmail parcel landed sploosh in the soft snow. "Whoever this fly boy is, he is really good," smiled Homer. Circling above him right now was the rescue plane that would get him out of this vast wilderness. Giddiness was tugging at Homer's heart. Like a playful cub wolf, he was wanting to jump and roll in the snow.

"Life is great," Homer discovered. Suddenly the motor of the small aircraft cut out; dead silence. Homer was horrified, his plane ticket out of here had lost power. Messages to rescue parties would not be carried on this wide winged bird. It was coming down and there was no clear place to land! This had to be the worst day of his life.

Then a strong, calm ethereal message cut through the cold Northern silence. "Stay where you are," came the descending words. "I will be back... Wave one hand if you understand, two hands if you do not."

Restraining himself from jumping up and down and waving both hands in the air jubilantly towards this heavenly preserver, Homer kept both fatigued arms by his side. Rising from his humble position with the help of his walking staff, Bill gave the appropriate one arm wave. Engine fired up again the motor drone was gradually fading, as the small plane disappearing into the distance left everything quiet and lonely again.

Obviously the retrieved package had been used as part of a makeshift survival packet. Contained in the small fire-blackened tin was coffee and stuffed in along side the Nabob packet was some candy bars, cigarettes and matches. A note signed by the owner, lay on top of the precious goods.

"I can't raise Fort Nelson on the radio," the note said. Bill knew about that. "I'll have to phone them from Trutch Lodge," finished the message. Building a tripod whittled from willow the men hung the container by the wire handle. A quickly built fire under the tin was melting snow soon after the plane had left.

Luckily Homer had the 'Milepost' with him. Stuck in a little village way out in the bush, with no cigarettes, at least he was not going to be left without something to read. Trutch Lodge, m. 200, fbks. 1327 miles north. Reading on, he noticed an Anderson was running information on local hunting at Mile 147, read Homer. "Must be where the pilot reigns from" he thought. Why with that little 'Cub' a man would have to be blind not to know where the game were roaming.

Meanwhile Jimmy carried on to touch down at Tuchodi Lakes. Pulling up close to the secure stash at the base camp, Jimmy proceeded to pack dry goods into the raised warehouse, wondering where the Beatty kid was hiding while the unloading was being done. A note attached to the cabin door initiated a ten minute flight up the Tuchodi

LOG OF ALASKA HIGHWAY

M. 147 (Fbks. 1380)—Beatton River Lodge—to the left, northbound, with meals, cabins, rooms, tub and shower baths, and a general merchandise store, including raw and finished furs for sale. Car service includes gas and oil—B.A. and affiliated credit cards, garage with heated storage, tires, complete repairs, towing and special hauling service. Information on local hunting and fishing. This is also the Pink Mountain P.O. Owned and operated by Jim and Lila Anderson.

MILEPOST 148 (Fbks. 1379)—Emergency flight strip No. 2.

MILEPOST 154 (Fbks. 1373)—Highway enters the Pink Mountains.

MILEPOST 161.8 (Fbks. 1365.2)—Sikanni Chief Hill, river & bridge. A picture opportunity.

MILEPOST 163 (Fbks. 1364)—Sikanni highway maintenance camp.

M. 170 (Fbks. 1357)—The beginning of the ascent to the summit of Trutch Mountain. Some good camera shots on this grade.

M. 171 (Fbks. 1356)—Mason Creek Lodge—operating a cafe, and rooms or cabins, grocery store and trailer space. Car service includes gas and oil, with B.A. and affiliated credit cards honored, lubrication, tires and general repairs, and limited warm storage, open 24 hours. Now under new management of the McGuire family.

MILEPOST 175.3 (Fbks. 1351.7)—Buckinghorse River and bridge.

M. 191 (Fbks. 1336)—The summit of Trutch Mountain, second highest point of the highway, elevation 4134 feet.

MILEPOST 195 (Fbks. 1332)—High panoramic view of northern Rockies.

M. 200 (Fbks. 1327)—Trutch Lodge, on the long crest of the summit of Trutch Mountain, with a coffee shop, general merchandise, rooms adjacent to tub, shower and modern plumbing, and service station. This spot has a fine panoramic view of some of the best game areas of this mountain region, and the owner, who is a "Class A" licensed guide, will arrange for hunting parties seeking Stone sheep, Grizzly bear, Caribou, Goat, and Moose. First class pack train and camping equipment are maintained here for sportsmen and hunting and fishing licenses are sold. Mail inquiries are solicited. Owned and operated by Mr. and Mrs. Don Peck.

M. 200.1 (Fbks. 1326.9)—Trutch maintenance camp and repeater station (public telephone and telegraph). Road information.

Valley. The letter was dated a week ago yesterday.

After three days of waiting out the weather for a plane ride, the camp attendant had decided to go ice fishing. As Jimmy had figured, the Beatty kid was getting tired of eating fish and the catching was not as exciting any more either. Enthusiastically he threw his camp gear together and climbed into the back of the Savage as soon as it landed. One more short stop at the Tuchodi main cabin, to collect the rest of his gear and then they would continue on to Trutch Lodge to unload the Beatty kid and pick up Gary Vince. Gary was interested in purchasing his own plane and wanted to know how difficult it would be to get in and out of his hunting territories by aircraft. While at Trutch Jimmy would phone D.O.T. and let them know where their missing sheep had strayed. That done he would then fly Gary out to his hunting cabins on the Muskwa.

FORMAL REPORTING

"What do you mean there is no plane down! I seen it myself," exclaimed Jimmy in frustration. "I was talking to them, damn it."

"There cannot be a plane down, we show nothing flying in that area," replied the confident voice at the other end of the phone.

"Well if you guys don't want them, I'll go get them myself," finished Jimmy.

"Just a minute Mr. Anderson," stated the official sounding voice. "We do have a suspended flight from Watson Lake, a U.S. craft has not yet arrived." Hesitation. "This could not be the one you have seen sir," doubted the Flight Service Specialist, "it is way too far south and miles out west," the qualified official informed the bush pilot. "Not even close to the flight route this craft would have been

117

flying," he affirmed. "However we will handle the sighting shortly Mr. Anderson!"

Hanging up the phone and turning to Gary Vince, Jimmy said. "Those Government cowboys said they would look after this here little show, but if those Yankee fly boys are not picked up by the time we get back from your cabins, we'll go bring-em back ourselves," promised Jimmy.

SMOKE BREAK

Hoping to buy acceptable smokes in Fort Nelson the men had elected to stretch their American cigarettes. Refusing the comfort of the tempting coffin nail retrieved from the rescue tin, Bill was briefly recounting his promises to a semi believing Homer. Sticking the Export plain to his lips, Homer admitted that a day of not smoking combined with the steady exercise and fresh air had made the young trekker's lungs fairly pure and healthy. Huge amounts of clean fresh dry air had been sucked deeply into the detoxified lungs, propelling the hikers onward. Homer admittedly was breathing a little better lately. But personally he had made no promises to any kind of a higher being, to be rescued. Boy, this North country? Would he ever be glad to get back to Missouri!

Scratching a kitchen sized wooden match across the face of a sun warmed rock Homer touched the flame to the cigarette tip. Deeply inhaling the flame of the Eddy match through the commercial Canadian weed, Homer felt the wrath, not of God but of RJR MacDonald's, export plain Cigarette. Woody, dry, rasping smoke hit Homer's young, fresh, northern air cleaned lungs with a violent choking reaction. Instantly the tissue destroying smoke was discarded with a fit of coughing in favour of the snow water, starting to form in the bottom of the fire coloured can.

Boiling snow for coffee was turning out to be quite a

feat in the small tin, but the well fed fire would soon produce hot water for the ground Java beans. Hunger pains had been satisfied by the chocolate bars and Homer's need for a smoke had been taken care of. Things were starting to shape up. What Homer needed now was a coffee and he had drank up all the water they had melted so far.   The water was finally starting to boil when the Cub glided over again.

"Sandbar, four miles ahead, think I can land." Yelled the pilot over the whistle of the air flowing through his open cockpit door. Power house of the Savage shut down, Jimmy was gliding over the two men on his way from Trutch to Gary's place.

"Which way?" shouted Bill, shrugging his shoulders. The pilot pointed and yelled.

"That way!" and firing up the plane, before losing too much altitude; kept right on going.

Regretfully, the tired men put out the fire. Picking up the dropped survival stash, they started walking the four miles to rescue. Things were looking a lot better, Homer's stressed body was just starting to relax. Nursing a parched throat, he carried the half tin of warm water. He was still needing a cup of coffee real bad, he was almost irate. Snow water was just starting to bubble in the pot when, Jimmy and his 'Angel Wings' showed up.

"I can land on that little island I sent them guys to with two passengers," Jimmy explained to Gary over the drone of the motor, "but I cannot take off with that much weight, he added. "There is no way I can land and take just one. To leave one by himself alone in their probable mental state would be dangerous," the bush pilot declared. "What we can do is land on the sandbar; I'll take one fellow out while you stay and look after the second guy. When I get back from

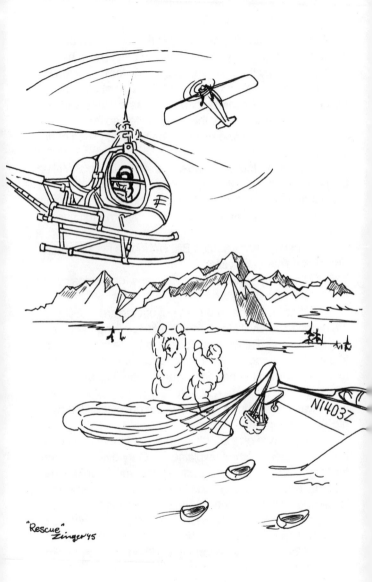

"Rescue"
Zinger '45

N1403Z

squaring up the first one with Peck at Trutch, I can fly the other to safety well before dark. Once we get those two out of the bush, I'll come back and get you." Jimmy knew he could leave Vince in the bush most any time by himself as long as needed and Gary would make out all right.

Climbing down a cliff, the two hikers finally reached the river. Walking through a swamp, they were constantly fighting off unbelievable hordes of mosquitoes. Down by the river there was a breeze and miraculously the insects disappeared. Continually sucking at the leather flight boots, the river turned to mud. Gumbo strained to stay attached to tired feet. "We have been in Muskeg: snow: rocks: cliffs: mud: water and ice," said Homer to himself. "All we missed was desert sand!"

Making their way along the river the men found a shallow place where the ice was solid. So as not to break through, they carefully slid across to a sandbar which formed a little island out in the middle of the river. Bill built another fire to begin heating water for coffee...again.

"What time is it?" asked Homer.

"Oh . . . I don't know," replied Bill. Time didn't mean much any more.

RESCUE

It was mid-afternoon by the time a guy came over in a stagger wing Beach or a Rocko. Bill couldn't tell. He was heating coffee. The D.O.T. aircraft came over real low and buzzed the men shortly after their cup of coffee. Following shortly was a helicopter, sent from a local oil company to pick Bill and Homer up. Hovering over to the downed T-34 they retrieved their scant gear and the registration and custom papers from the damaged Mentor's cockpit, Bill figured he would need these.

CANADA

DEPARTMENT OF TRANSPORT

AIR SERVICES
CIVIL AVIATION BRANCH

Serial No. F-239

ACCIDENT REPORT

Aircraft: Beechcraft T34, N1403Z
Place: 13 miles east of Kluachesi Lake, B.C. (Lat. 57°58'N; Long. 123°38'W)
Date: 7th May, 1961.   1115 hours

SUMMARY   All Times are Pacific Standard

On 7th May 1961, W. Hickinbotham was pilot-in-command of Beechcraft T34 aircraft, registration N1403Z, operated by the Elmendorf Air Force Base Aero Club in Alaska. One passenger, H. Perkins, was also on board.

At about 1115 hours, a precautionary landing was made due to deteriorating weather and shortage of fuel.

The occupants were not injured but the aircraft was substantially damaged.

INVESTIGATION

A Certificate of Airworthiness had been issued for the aircraft. There was no evidence to indicate any fault in the airframe, engine, propeller or controls prior to the accident.

The pilot held a Private Pilot Licence and his total flying experience was 450 hours. He had flown 15 hours on the Beechcraft T34 aircraft, all within the 90 days prior to the accident.

On the 6th May the aircraft landed on the Alaska Highway at Mile 408 in deteriorating weather. It departed at about 0900 hours on 7th May to continue the flight to Fort Nelson, B.C. under anticipated VFR conditions.

The aircraft entered a mountain pass under an overcast. Snow began to fall, decreasing the forward visibility and obscuring the pilots view of the ground as it covered the highway. He decided to climb through the overcast and having done so, he flew toward Fort Nelson using the low frequency radio range. He was unable to establish communication with Fort Nelson on any frequency.

The pilot reported that after passing Fort Nelson a descent was made through the overcast, clear of the range leg. The visibility below the overcast was reported to be good but the pilot was unable to establish his position. The fuel supply was so reduced at this point that a wheels down landing was made near a tractor trail in an area relatively clear of trees.

The nose undercarriage assembly was broken and dents were made in the leading edges of both wings. The propeller and right wing tip were damaged.

A general forecast from three reporting stations in the area and during the period of the flight was for a cloud base of 8000 feet with visibility 30 miles in very light snow showers. The pilot was not aware of this forecast, and his only information on the weather was obtained from passing motorists on the Alaska Highway. The weather that the pilot encountered is considered to have been a local condition which existed in the mountain pass. An aftercast of the weather showed the weather to be generally as forecast.

CONCLUSION

The flight was continued into unfavourable weather. The pilot became lost and was compelled to land in an unsuitable area.

Returning from Gary's hunting cabins, Jimmy flew over the crash site to check on things. A Stagger wing Beechcraft piloted by Jim Burros, was flying a mother hen pattern over the rescue operation. Jimmy made a high pass. Thinking the Savage might land, the helicopter lifted up and moved over. Precious daylight flight time already robbed from a tight agenda, created by the previous week of bad flying conditions, made landing time scarce. A few feet off the deck, with engine cut, the Savage was again gliding over the American survivors. Through the opening of the cabin door the bush pilot said. "You got'er built there buddy, we'll see you later." With that said the Super Cub fired up and faded off into the distance towards Peck's Trutch Lodge.

Flying the weathered men back to the safety and comfort of the Fort Nelson Hotel, the helicopter pilot commented. "Thirteen miles east of Kluachesi Lake, Lat. 57" 58'N; Long. 123" 38'W: One-hundred miles Southwest of Fort Nelson, you guys could have been out here a while." Homer was smiling as he nodded his head in agreement, he was quite happy to be, once more, airborne.

The faint smell of shampoo, was overridden by smoke and bush smell still radiating from the soaked flight gear, now lying in a heap in the far corner of the hotel room. Slipping blistered feet into fresh socks obtained from his travel bag, Bill marvelled at how good it felt to be clean. Hobbling down to the dining room in borrowed slippers, the men were served by an eager waiter who asked.

"What would you like mister? Would you like a steak?"

"No Sir." replied Bill, "I would like to have frankfurters and beans."

"What?" questioned the waiter.

"You know it's just possible out there with perhaps

snare cable from the T-34, we might have been able to get a steak somehow," answered Bill. "Frankfurters and beans we could not have got, and to me, are a sign of civilization. . . And I think I would like frankfurters and beans!" After a meal of frankfurters and beans the men reported to the Department Of Transport. Bill made out all the reports for the D. O. T. and for the FU, (U. S. navigation administration).

Later, Bill called Jimmy by telephone. He thanked Jimmy profusely for saving him and Homer's life. Bill, when passing on wishes of good health to the parent's of his preserver, regrettably was informed that Lila, who had survived Jim senior by almost two years, had passed away this spring on April 5th. Exactly one month before the men left on their fateful flight.

Time did not permit a meeting with the Canadian bush pilot as the D. O. T. was already arranging rides for the two men with a transport plane going through to Whitehorse. Bill circled the mile 147 advertisement in Homer's Milepost. Someday he would personally meet this man every one seemed to know and refer to as 'Midnight'.

From Whitehorse the rescued men would be boarding a Pan Am Airline to Fairbanks, Alaska. The last hop from Fairbanks, to Anchorage Alaska, would be getting them back home the next afternoon. Elmendorf Aero Flight Club had been notified of the Tech Sergeant's plight and upon arrival, Bill was examined and questioned by an Inspector about the incident in great length.

Homer left Anchorage heading to Seattle again two days later, this time it was in a larger aircraft. He was not taking any chances, this flight was going to get him home. Homer had a real Northern story for the folks back in Missouri.

The United States Air Force sent a Sikorsky helicopter down from Anchorage and staging the recovery operation out of Fort Nelson, the T-34 Beechcraft was airlifted by helicopter to the Fort Nelson Airport. After straightening the prop a bit and attaching the root of the nose landing gear to the aircraft the T-34 was ready to fly again. With the right wing tip spruced up a bit, the Elmendorf flying club relayed the T-34 back to it's home base in Alaska. Cost of the repair job, eight-hundred dollars. Not too bad for a bush landing!

Four years later, in April of l965, Bill was driving up to Anchorage from Los Angeles and stopping at mile 147 was pleased to find Jimmy operating the Pink Mountain Lodge. He was just finishing a large burnt wood mural on the cafe wall. "He's really a talented guy," thought Bill.

"Jimmy you know, the only thing about this is," said

"Jimmy
Merry Christmas
Bill

The Card. Unger 95.

Bill. "I have been re-flying that flight every night in my sleep, for the last four years," he confessed. "Thinking,.. If I just had not got up that morning... If I had not done this or if I had not done that or. . . And . . . I always have questions. What if you had never shown up?" He speculated. "What then??"

"What you did was exactly right," the veteran bush pilot said with great conviction, while looking Bill square in the eye.

If you had done it any other way," stated Jimmy. "You could have, damn easily, still been out there somewhere."

"Should I have tried for the Fort Nelson airstrip?" inquired Bill. "Or at least the Alcan Highway!" Jimmy resting his hand on Bill's shoulders said.

"Listen buds you're alive," affirmed Jimmy. "You did every thing right; you guys came out alive," he sanctioned. "Up here that's what counts! Do you understand what I'm saying?" questioned Midnight.

That day was one of the most meaningful experiences of Bill's life. It was as if a weight had been lifted from his shoulders. He could only liken it to meeting his Saviour because, in a sense, the bush pilot was Bill's SECOND Saviour.

Bill knew the Lord saved his soul that day in May of 1961, and this northern bush pilot, and his 'Angel Wings', saved his life.

Every year on May 8th Bill would be sending a Christmas card to "Jimmy 'Midnight' Anderson, Pink Mountain Post Office." Alaska Highway, BC.

Bill was convinced that if this man, call it divine intervention if you will, hadn't changed the course of his flight that day, Bill would never have experienced another Christmas. Period.

Ex-United States Staff Sergeant Bill Hickinbothem, now totally blind, is still fulfilling his promise to God. Travelling clear over to North Dakota and back down into Texas, the travelling Anglican minister's territory also includes the last state of the union. While travelling through to Alaska, Bill, also visits churches in parts of British Columbia. Vividly he remembers when his life was restarted the moment the crew of the T-34 envisioned a beautiful sight of 'Angel wings' carrying a northern bush pilot called:

Jimmy 'Midnight' Anderson.

The End

Jimmy *"Midnight"* Anderson

BUSH PILOTS   **MILE 148**
ROOST   **ALASKA HWY**

PINK MOUNTAIN, BC, V0C 2B0

Phone: None   **Fax: Get Serious**